SOLDIER OF FORTUNE 8

TARGET THE DEATH-DEALER

SOLDIER OF FORTUNE 8

TARGET THE DEATH-DEALER

Robin James

Para Maria del Mar Pomares Torres, con todo mi cariño. Muchos besos.

First published in Great Britain 1995
22 Books, Invicta House, Sir Thomas Longley Road,
Rochester, Kent

Copyright © 1995 by 22 Books

The name Robin James is a pen-name of James Hallums

The moral right of the author has been asserted

A CIP catalogue record for this book is available from the
British Library

ISBN 1 898125 36 8

10 9 8 7 6 5 4 3 2 1

Typeset by Hewer Text Composition Services, Edinburgh
Printed in Great Britain by Cox and Wyman Limited, Reading

1

London was wet. It was June and it was raining lightly, which was about par for the course. Outside Crockford's in Curzon Street, Mayfair, a frail, elderly American lady with rock-solid purple hair was ducking from a taxi to beneath the shelter of the uniformed doorman's candy-striped umbrella. As, a crabby hand on the small of her back and wincing with lumbar pain, she straightened, pushing her gold-framed spectacles to the bridge of her nose, the menace lingering in the shelter of a nearby doorway – a young man in jeans, trainers and a black windcheater – started his run.

A second taxi had parked almost simulta-neously behind the old lady's, its fares a ruggedly good-looking man in his mid-forties – though he might have been taken for thirty-eight or so – and a pretty, twenty-something girl. His business with the taxi driver done with, the man uncased his umbrella and opened his door. Sticking the umbrella out into the damp night, he pressed the button to open it. As it sprang to life and he planted a foot on the pavement, the young man rushed past.

There was a squeal of pain and outrage from the American lady as the bag-snatcher, barely slowing down, grabbed her deep-green, crocodile-skin handbag, dragging her into the arms of the doorman as he did so, and hared off down Cu:zon Street with his prize.

Stephen Forbes reacted with a speed which had not deserted him since his SAS and mercenary days. Dropping his umbrella in the gutter, he leapt from the taxi and charged off after the thief.

'Clown!' muttered the young lady, Leila, shaking her head at her husband's speedily retreating midnight-blue, Armani-suited back. She slid across the rear seat of the cab and leant out to retrieve the umbrella. The American lady was screaming hysterically as she disentangled herself from the reeling doorman.

The thief ducked around a corner and sprinted towards Shepherd Market. He was unaware that he was being chased since the evening traffic's grumble was loud and his pursuer was not – as most men in his situation would be – shouting; he knew that to do so would merely serve to bring a surge to the lad's already seething adrenalin and further speed to his feet.

Forbes kept himself in tip-top shape with regular, strenuous exercise, and despite the age difference he was closing in. Skidding into an alleyway, the young man shot a look over his shoulder and began to slow down. Panting heavily, he shoved the handbag inside his wind-cheater and decelerated to a fast walk. Forbes ran into the alley, where it was sheltered and quiet. The fast splashing of his Gucci shoes gave him away.

It was too late for the bag-snatcher to pick up sufficient speed to get away. The big man – six-two in his socks – was on him, bringing him crashing to the worn cobblestones with a rugby-style tackle. Kneeling over him, Forbes dragged the lad's hand behind his back and yanked his arm up in a half nelson, then struggled to his feet, bringing him up with him. 'The bag, kid,' he said flatly to the cowering, gasping teenager, whose nose and forehead were trickling blood which was being washed over his face by the drizzle.

One or two people, keeping a discreet distance, were beginning to take notice.

'Run,' said Forbes, the bag in his hand.

'What?'

'Piss off. Get out of here fast. You want the Bill on your back as well as me?'

He ran.

3

When her husband returned, triumphantly bearing the American woman's handbag, Leila was waiting with her, the two of them sheltering under the gambling club's porch. Forbes's short, neat brown hair with its greying temple areas was plastered to his squarish head, his suit was patchy with damp and there was a small tear in the knee of his right trouser leg from which blood was oozing.

'Gee, thanks,' said the woman as he gave her her bag. 'Hell, that wouldn't happen in a million years in Fort Lauderdale, someone getting involved like that.'

'Believe me,' Leila told her as she frowningly looked her husband up and down, appearing irritated while actually impressed, 'it doesn't happen in London, either. You got lucky, lady.'

'Maybe we'll all get lucky,' Forbes said. He took Leila by her Valentino-clad elbow and made to head her into the foyer. 'But first I need a stiff drink.'

The American stopped them. Dipping into her bag, she produced a handful of twenty-dollar bills. 'Listen, maybe I can ... ?' she began, offering the money to Forbes.

He interrupted her, pushing her hand away. 'Forget it. Old-fashioned British hospitality.'

'Oh. What happened to the thief? Did he ... ?'

Again he cut in. 'He got away.'

'Pity.'

'You let him go, didn't you?' asked Leila as, minus the woman, they settled on to cream leather-topped stools in Crockford's luxurious bar. Forbes smiled at her, dabbing his knee through the tear with a handkerchief; it was only a slight graze; but for the wetness the bleeding would already have stopped. 'Sure I did. I'm not a great lover of the boys in blue, you know that. Anyhow, with luck he's learnt his lesson. He won't be mugging little old ladies again.'

'Fat chance.'

He grinned. 'Not in front of me, he won't.' He ordered himself a triple Ballantine's, on the rocks with just a dash of soda, and a martini for Leila.

'Remind me again what we're doing here?' Leila said as she sipped her drink. 'Why we're spending a long weekend in a suite at the Savoy – a suite, no less; you couldn't just take a room – eating at Quaglino's and are about to gamble with the last of our bread? It kind of scares me.'

His steely-blue, slightly cynical eyes crinkled with amusement at the edges as he gazed lovingly into hers, soft-brown, wide-spaced and droopy. You are so lovely, little wife, he thought. 'Scared?' he said. 'You? Pull the other one.'

Forbes's scepticism was fully justified. For

five foot two Leila, with her shoulder-length, burnt-umber hair and her cute little nose with a freckle near its tip, was – outwardly at least – fearless. Palestinian by birth, now British by nationality, at the tender age of sixteen, having been fully trained in Libya and a member of the terrorist group Al Fatah, Leila had once helped hijack an airbus. And just two years ago she had aided Forbes to plan, put into action and then to thwart – for reasons most devious – the robbery of a colossal amount of Saudi Arabian gold ingots from a London bank. And since then the two of them had been living the life of Reilly on the two-million-dollar reward from the Saudi government.

'I *was* scared once,' she said. 'The day we got hitched.'

He laughed, chucking her defiant little chin. 'Rightly so, kid. Old man like me.'

'Not so old. The way you just sprinted down Curzon Street. Christ.' She studied his worldly-wise face with its little scar on one cheek which seemed to have been carefully placed by some make-up artist in order to enhance his tough good looks. Scared she wasn't, but troubled, she was. 'You really want to risk the last of our capital?' she asked him. '*All* of it?'

'All seventeen K, yeah.'

Incredibly, after two years of riotous living, of travelling the world first class together in their new status of husband and wife, of staying in the very best hotels, of buying a country retreat in Wiltshire and of making two seriously ill-advised investments, £17,000 in cash was all they had left from two million dollars; that and their expensive clothes and jewellery and the Wiltshire cottage. Mr and Mrs Stephen Forbes were, by their standards at any rate, flat broke. They were also unemployed – a couple the London police would describe as having no 'visibles' – and, except in certain, very specialized departments, they were more or less unemployable. Meanwhile, here they were, sitting at the bar of Crockford's in their beautifully made, expensive clothes – his designer suit bedraggled and with a tear in its right knee – with £17,000 in cash on them.

Neither of them had been seduced by the credit-card habit. Stephen Forbes wanted no computerized records of his financial transactions and Leila simply loved the feel of cash and the pleasure of spending it; in Leila's handbag there nestled two hundred fifty-pound notes, while in the two inside pockets of Forbes's suit there were one hundred and forty more. In reserve in the safe in their suite at the Savoy was a further £5000, but that sum was little more than they would need to meet current expenses.

'Let's do it,' said Forbes. He downed the last of his whisky, the good, clean spirit spreading warmth through his stomach, bolstering his confidence. 'We hit one table after the other, playing high stakes. If we get lucky we raise to the limit, and press. And press.'

'At least we're going to have fun to the bitter end.' Leila's eyes smiled at her husband over the rim of her glass, but she did not appear exactly over the moon with happiness.

'We either walk out of here with half a million quid, or' – he slipped off his barstool – '. . . we go out with zilch.'

Leila wriggled her enchanting little backside against the stool leather as she finished her martini. Zilch I'm afraid it's going to be, lover, she was thinking, but she said: 'And if we do happen to leave here boracic, you visit the man on Monday morning, right?'

'Amazing the slang you pick up.' He helped her to stand; she was wearing gold, four-inch-heeled shoes. 'I keep my appointment at the Kuwaiti embassy. Right.'

The purple-coiffed American lady was sitting at the *chemin de fer* table. She was losing heavily, betting into a running bank which a man of Arab appearance, his swarthy features inscrutable, was letting run without garaging – that is, without setting part of his winnings safely to one side. While Forbes and Leila watched, the dealer called '*Neuf à la banque*' – an unbeatable nine for the Arab – four times. With a pile of chips worth £30,000 heaped in the centre of the table – at least a third of them won from the old lady – the Arab decided his bank had had its run and he passed it. The next player opened with only one hundred pounds. The American covered it and again lost.

'I should have left the kid alone,' Forbes observed mildly. 'She's going to blow the lot anyway.'

One of the nine seats was free for the next shoe. Leila took it and bet according to Forbes's instructions, only to lose £1500 in twenty minutes.

It was more or less the same story playing roulette: they constantly guessed the numbers and colours wrong, then two blackjack dealers seemed to take a vindictive dislike to them. But around midnight, with only a few thousand pounds left between them, their luck started to turn. They had switched to the recently installed craps table. Forbes was the shooter, bouncing the transparent, red precision dice with cool enthusiasm – plus a certain amount of affection – over the green baize cloth. He was hitting all the right numbers, letting his bets – on the Come line, the Pass line and, when he failed to hit a natural seven or eleven on the first roll, the number he needed – ride.

As always, whenever there is a hot roller on the craps table, the news spread fast. Forbes's winning streak attracted the attention of a boisterous crowd of regular gamblers, who began to bet along with him. It was hitting the house hard, and a fever of greedy excitement crackled in the air. Reaching the house limit, he played on at maximum stakes, pocketing a heavy profit for himself and his followers as the management tried to kill his luck by three times changing the stickman. When he finally rolled a first-time losing combination of two and one, for the first time Forbes counted his chips; they totalled approximately £34,000.

The couple moved on, this time to the high-stake baccarat table, where the odds were only very slightly – less than one per cent – in favour of the house. From Crockford's point of view it was their most dangerous game. Here it would be possible for a punter – admittedly given extraordinary luck – to convert £34,000 into half a million.

They actually topped the two hundred thousand mark, by which time they were both fighting with nerves stretched tauter than piano wires; this money business was more gut-wrenching than being involved in a commando raid. Many a more prudent couple would have cashed in at that stage and left. Not them – at least not Stephen Forbes. On her own, Leila might have, but she was happy to let her piss-on-the-devil husband take the decisions, and she was certainly not about to nag him to call it a night. Besides, her nervous system might have been going through merry hell, but the constant rush of excitement was making her as light-headed as if she had been toking Acapulco Gold all evening; she was floating on a massive high with it.

Five hundred thousand quid, Forbes had vowed, and there was no way he was going to walk out of Crockford's with a penny less. It was that princely sum or nothing.

An hour and three quarters later they were walking all right – through persistent rain – in the direction of the Savoy. In fact they did have the money to pay a taxi; they had more – about £150. But for some insane reason dispirited Stephen Forbes felt like getting thoroughly wet and Leila was not averse to the idea either.

Subdued and brooding, they said little. Deflated

they might be, but it was not in the basically sunny nature of either of them to let depression settle in. After all, tomorrow was the first day of the rest of their lives – and Forbes was going back into business.

2

Irritation was seeping all the way into his bones, causing him to constantly fidget. The sun that morning had made the effort to dribble through thin cloud cover, and Forbes had elected to walk the almost two miles from the Savoy to the Kuwaiti Embassy at 45–46 Queensgate, cutting through Green Park on his way, enjoying its fresh, greeny, after-rain smells. The losses of the previous night were behind him, easily forgotten past history; what the hell, he and Leila could hardly have kept high-kicking on peanuts.

He had arrived at the embassy one and a half minutes early for his appointment, at just before eleven. It was now ten minutes to twelve and he was still waiting. He was doing his fidgeting in a room, with its heavy, red and green, fancy flock wallpaper, its thick red carpet and ornate chandeliers, that would have served better as a nightclub. He should of course have expected this treatment, he told himself. He had dealt with goddam Arabs many times in the past and they had invariably kept him waiting; it was part of their nature. Nevertheless, had his business not been so vital he might well have left.

At three minutes after twelve a poker-faced menial stuck his hooky nose around the huge Victorian door and in an ostentatiously grand manner informed Forbes that the ambassador would see him.

'Well, that is fucking good of him,' Forbes muttered to the man's black-jacketed back as he followed it along a windowless, eighteen-foot-high, neon-lit passageway.

'Come in, Mr Forbes, do,' said the ambassador. 'Welcome.' Khalet Awadi was a tall, skinny individual wearing a dark-grey suit and with a neatly trimmed, jet-black beard and moustache. Dark, probing eyes glinted behind thick-lensed, gold-rimmed spectacles. There was no attempt at an apology from him, but then Forbes had not for a second expected one. The ambassador at least had the manners to have risen behind his over-ornate rococo desk and waved a heavily gold-ringed hand at a green-velvet, high-backed chair in front of it. 'Sit down, please.'

Awadi scrutinized Forbes carefully. The Englishman was neatly dressed in pale-beige trousers and a navy-blue, double-breasted Burberry blazer and a White's Club tie to which he was not entitled. During some twenty seconds of silence

Forbes's eyes moved from the other man to a paper flattened on his desk and back again. Then the ambassador slid an open silver box towards him. 'Cigarette?'

'No.'

He lit a cigarette for himself, after carefully inserting it in a slender silver holder. Then he said, reading from the piece of paper: 'Stephen Francis Forbes. Born 24 May 1948. Dropped out of school aged sixteen to become a car salesman. Joined the regular British Army June 1966, served five years, then entered the SAS. Achieved rank of lieutenant before resigning aged twenty-nine to become a mercenary. Mike Hoare's right-hand man in the Congo before leading his own band in West Africa, then in Nicaragua. In 1992 masterminded a spectacular robbery of Saudi Arabian gold in London, finally turning the gold over to the Saudis themselves in return for a substantial reward.'

The ambassador's shrewd eyes slid to grab those of the man whose life he had so baldly outlined and who had not moved a muscle of his face during the little speech. 'Nothing known since. Quite a history, Mr Forbes.'

Forbes was not filled with happiness; this sort of information about his private life was why he avoided credit cards and bank accounts. 'Chased a young tea leaf in the rain along Curzon Street at ten twenty-five last night, retrieved an old American lady's snatched handbag,' he said drily. 'You seem to have overlooked that.'

Awadi mouthed a smile, flashing a pair of gold teeth. 'Occasionally exhibits qualities more attributable to Joan of Arc than to the aforementioned Mike Hoare.'

'You also forgot my years of dealings – totally legitimate – in the Middle East.'

'I glossed over it. During which you discovered the existence of a secret stockpile of Saudi gold in Wigmore Street, in a bank vault. It's documented.' The bony hand clutching the cigarette-holder tapped on the sheet of paper. Ash sprinkled the red-leather desktop. 'I thought it wise not to over-bore you with yourself.'

Forbes recrossed his legs the other way round. 'What do you want?'

'You achieved the not inconsiderable feat of stealing Saudi gold. Do you think you're capable of hijacking a Saudi citizen?'

'The story being?'

'He's a sheikh – which fact in itself is of minor importance. It actually signifies little more than a tribal or village leader.'

'You don't have to tell me about the social structures of your race, Mr Awadi. I'm well aware of them.'

'His name is Sheikh Yasser Sulman. He is an

international arms dealer on a massive scale. He lives most of the time in Spain.'

'And you want him kidnapped. Let me guess why. He's supplying Iraq?'

'Is and was. Before and during the Gulf War. And now.'

'And the UN?' Forbes ran a hand over his smoothly shaved cheek. He had nicked it badly that morning with his razor; it had still been leaking a little blood just before he left and now he remembered he had neglected to remove its tiny speck of toilet paper. He did so. 'Aren't they interested? There's a total ban on supplying weapons to Saddam.'

'They have no proof. We have no proof — we know, that's all. If the UN had proof they would put pressure on Spain to hand him over. But even that might prove difficult since Sulman is held in some respect by the Spanish government. They do business with the man.'

'So. You want the sheikh desperately. To put an end to his trade, obviously, but also to find out what Saddam's present arms capability might be. Then, naturally, you'll kill him.'

The ambassador drew heavily on the ivory tip of his cigarette-holder, holding the smoke in, then letting it dribble out as he said: 'So far you've anticipated everything I was about to tell you. But we don't kill people, Mr Forbes.'

'You'll kill him.' He paused. 'Whereabouts in Spain does he hang out?'

'The south. Marbella.'

'In fine company. With all the British retired villains. I know it well.' He thought for a moment. 'How tight is his security?'

'I couldn't give you more than the roughest of ideas. It's for you to find out if you accept the commission. He has bodyguards, that I know. And they can be licensed to carry guns in that country.'

'I'm not for hire cheaply. And I'll need expensive, professional help.' Forbes switched on his most earnest expression. 'I'll get your sheikh for you.'

'We've no doubt you will. That's why we approached you.' Awadi stubbed out his cigarette and ejected it from its holder. He laid the holder down very carefully, levelling it up exactly with the edge of the sheet of paper with Forbes's life history scribbled on it. 'You will be paid when we get the desired result, when Sulman is in our hands, in Kuwait City.'

Forbes shook his head. 'I don't start the job without a down payment. Neither will my people. And there will be considerable expenses to be taken care of.'

'I suggest you get yourself down to Marbella and do a little research. One of my staff will be there to supply you with funds. When you know how many men you'll need we'll discuss their fee. In the meantime, if you agree, there's an advance of $50,000.' Opening a drawer, he produced from it a fat, manila envelope, which he pushed across the desk towards Forbes. 'It's all there.'

'It's only about half of what I dropped at Crockford's last night.' He did not touch it. 'And when I deliver the sheikh?'

The ambassador wrapped two knuckles on the envelope. 'That represents ten per cent.'

Forbes thought about his target in the casino the previous night. Half a million dollars was not far short of it; it was an excellent fee for what sounded like an easy job. Hell, he thought, go for it, boy, don't settle for less. 'Pounds, not dollars,' he said.

The dark eyes with their thick, curly lashes searched Forbes's face, looking for a weakness but finding none. 'Half a million dollars is more than adequate. I can get someone for far less.'

'But he won't be me. I'll guarantee you delivery.' He uncrossed his legs.

'Our offer is in dollars.'

The Englishman got to his feet. 'Every man has a price,' he said, firmly. 'Mine is in pounds. Half a million of them, preferably fresh off the press.' He tightened the knot in his White's tie.

'If you don't agree, then fine,' he bluffed. 'I have an alternative proposition.'

'I'll have to get the authority.'

Forbes raised an eyebrow. 'Then get it, my friend. You can reach me at my suite in the Savoy.'

3

'This clown is going to get right up my nostrils,' grumbled Forbes to Leila.

They were having breakfast on the terrace of their rented bungalow in the grounds of the Marbella Club Hotel. It was nine-fifteen on a sun-drenched morning and just two days since Khalet Awadi's agreement to Forbes's terms. One Hammid Mullah, accountant by profession and nature and in charge of looking after the Englishman's expenses during the Sulman operation, had just left them.

'Seems reasonable to me,' said Leila. 'Why should he pay for a hired Merc at a hundred and twenty-five quid a day when a little runabout at ten will do the job? Quibbling over peanuts when the deal's going to pan out at something over eight hundred grand. It's insane. If we're here two weeks and he's saved his country fifteen hundred quid in car hire he's earned his keep. He's happy. I wouldn't let him bug you, darling.'

Forbes had been spreading coarse-cut marmalade on a slice of toast heavy with butter. He sighed. 'Shit, you're right.' He bit into the toast. Chewing, he said: 'If I want a Merc I can pay for it myself.'

'I understood that this time around we were going to be a bit more careful breadwise?'

'You're right again. We'll take a Fiesta and let them pay.'

As she sipped coffee, Leila glanced around the pretty little garden. It was alive with birdsong, there was a small swimming pool, beds of fragrant, blooming roses – and there was a jacaranda tree, the dazzling purple of its leaves astonishingly beautiful. 'God, it's so lovely here,' she remarked. 'At least our friend Mullah didn't kick about the cost of this.'

'Seven hundred and fifty a day with breakfast,' said Forbes, producing a satisfied smile. 'He did and I told him where the Kuwaitis could stuff their job if we couldn't stay here. I've always stayed here when in Marbella – you know that. It provides a good cover, too. Only for the super-rich, not a toerag of an ex-mercenary.'

She giggled. 'Love ourself today, do we?'

Leaning across the wicker table he planted a kiss on her nose, on the freckle. 'To death, kid. Love myself every day. Love you more. Finish breakfast and we'll get to work.'

22

'We?'

'What do you think I brought you with me for when the place is crawling with willing chicks?'

An hour and a half later, not in a Ford Fiesta but one of the oddly named Renault Twingos – Leila thought it sounded like a chocolate bar – they were pulling off the N340, in the direction of the beach, twenty-one kilometres west of Marbella.

Ambassador Awadi had contrived to have a certain amount of research done; the hand-drawn map which Forbes had studied before leaving the Marbella Club and which Leila had open on her lap was neat and meticulous. It was an outline of an area one kilometre square; the bumpy track down which they were heading appeared in its far right-hand corner. It was a fairly bleak part of the coast, technically speaking not in the municipality of Marbella at all, but in that of Estepona. There were two small pine woods, an *atalaya* – one of the semi-ruined Moorish watch-towers which are in sight of one another all along the Spanish beaches – and a couple of farmhouses plus some rickety animal shelters. Occupying the left-hand corner of the map was the house of the target, Sheikh Yasser Sulman, a massive villa named Casa al-Riyadh. The rest, as far as Forbes and Leila could see from the track, was rolling, scrubby grass fields with a little cultivation and some pigs and donkeys.

According to the map, the sheikh's palatial villa was sitting amid something like thirty thousand square metres of gardens. It was almost a kilometre distant from them, and they could only see the top of its green-tiled turret.

Leila was driving. Reaching the beach, she parked the Twingo – more or less the same colour as the jacaranda in the bungalow garden, but lurid on a car – among some grass-tufted dunes. There were a few other cars scattered around, which suited Forbes's purpose since he preferred that there would be some people on the beach.

Leila unclipped her flared white mini skirt and stepped out of it. She unbuttoned her lilac blouse; beneath it she was wearing a tiny, pink bikini. Forbes stripped to blue swimming shorts and a pair of espadrilles. He hung a pair of Leitz binoculars around his neck, and a Nikon camera with a 400mm telephoto lens attached. Then he draped a brightly patterned towel over a shoulder, pulled low over his forehead a blue cotton fisherman's hat with the words 'Costa del Sol' in white splashed on it and put on a pair of big sunglasses with dayglo yellow frames.

Leila laughed at him. 'You look like a prize bloody grockle,' she said.

'That's the general idea. I feel like one. It isn't pleasant.' He ran his eyes over her in appreciation. 'But you don't exactly look like a grockle's girlfriend.' On the contrary: with her curvaceous little body all but exposed and that lustrous hair cascading over her shoulders she was a delectable dream. She hooked some small, silver-framed sunglasses over her ears and took a towel from the car. 'Shouldn't you be wearing some sort of shoes?' Forbes asked her.

'You know how tough my feet are. The soles are like leather.'

It was true. Barefoot training in Libya all those years before had hardened them and ever since then a habit of being without shoes wherever and whenever possible had helped keep them that way.

'At some point we'll be coming off the beach,' said Forbes.

'It's OK,' Leila insisted.

In the south of Spain June tends to be one of the most agreeable months of the year. The sun tans nicely without reaching the sweltering heat of midsummer, and there is generally a cooling, pleasant edge to the breeze. Today was one of those days. The Mediterranean sparkled as if afloat with clusters of diamonds as it threw long, lazy waves on to the beach.

As Forbes and Leila began to stroll hand

in hand along the sand they saw that the owners of the cars parked among the dunes had occupied their little bits of territory at widely spaced intervals. They soon discovered why. Walking in the direction of Sulman's villa – Forbes with his shoes in his hand, their feet sinking into wet sand and every now and then covered with surf – they approached the first of the sun worshippers; they were two girls, as brown as walnuts, stretched out on their backs naked, their bodies glistening with oil. Their legs were slightly apart, their eyes closed. As Forbes and Leila passed within a metre of the pair, between the sea and them, Forbes's gaze was irresistibly drawn to their crotches.

Leila tugged hard on his hand. 'Oi!' she said, loudly enough to cause one of the girls to open her eyes – though she did nothing about closing her legs.

'Pussy. What do you expect?' muttered Forbes with a happy grin.

A little further along the beach, Leila got her own back. As they passed a nude couple – the man muscular, young, reading a newspaper – she inspected his genitals with a little smile. 'Oh, wow!' she whispered. 'Hung like a donkey. Ooo!'

Laughing, he pulled her to him and kissed her on the lips. 'Bitch.'

She broke away from him, took off her bikini top and started to pull down the bottom.

'What the hell . . . ?'

'When in Rome.' She stepped out of the pants.

'We happen to be here to do a specific job of work.'

'Which entails us appearing to be people having innocent fun on a beach, remember?' She stared pointedly at his trunks. 'Off.'

He grunted and obeyed.

'Not quite as well hung as our friend there, but you'll do.'

'I'll kill you.'

She studied him. Nude, but with his ridiculous hat and sunglasses, the multi-coloured towel, binoculars and camera around his neck, and shoes and shorts in his hands, he presented a particularly odd sight. 'You look more like a grockle than a grockle.'

Twenty minutes later, when they had left the last of the naked sunbathers behind and were nearing the bottom of the garden of Casa al-Riyadh, not wishing to provoke undue attention from any guards who might be watching from the house they put their swimwear back on.

The only part of the villa actually visible was the turret. A three-metre-high, heavy chain-link fence ran the three hundred metres from the front of the garden to the beach, where it made a right angle to carry on along the hundred metres or so of beach frontage. The first thing that caught Forbes's eye as they approached the corner was a large Smith's Electronics security camera fixed to the top of the fence pole. The second was another fence, within the first, ten metres away from it and running parallel. Focusing his Nikon on a farmhouse to the west of the villa, he snapped it then swung the camera to take two rapid shots of the fence and security camera.

Laughing and joking with one another, every inch holidaymakers, they wandered right up to the fence, snapping pictures of each other with it in the background.

From where they were, there was very little to see. An immaculately tended lawn tumbled down from a height of about twenty metres to the edge of the inner fence. The house was set way back at the front end of the garden, invisible, even its turret out of sight.

The peace of the day was shattered. Three Rottweilers with smooth black coats and docked tails came haring towards Forbes and Leila between the fences, jaws slavering, kicking up as much racket as a pack of howling wolves. There was no way the killer dogs could get at them – though had there been they would surely have ripped them to shreds – but they presented such a fearsome sight that their would-be victims backed hurriedly away from the fence.

'Dog run,' said Forbes. 'What I thought it was. The man is sure as hell scared of something.'

They moved back into the edge of the sea and went splashing on in an easterly direction as the dogs barked ceaselessly, following them, hurling themselves at the fence.

'We are, of course, being most carefully watched,' observed Forbes as they reached the far corner of the garden. That corner post, too, was topped with a security camera. Taking Leila into his arms, he pressed his lips on to hers, kissing her with passion and bending at the knees so that his stirring crotch was pressed into hers while he tried to keep the camera and binoculars from digging into her.

His hand crept into the back of her bikini bottom to squeeze a buttock. She wriggled against him for a second, then pushed herself away. 'I don't reckon we ought to *do* that, lover,' she told him. 'Not if we're on the telly.'

He agreed with reluctance. He was tense with excitement at the task before him, the excitement keen now that he was right here, outside the fortress of a home of the man he was bent on kidnapping; the fact that his beloved Leila was with him was catalysing that excitement into sexual arousal. Such things happened to him. Trying to dismiss the difficult-to-ignore condition, he took Leila by the hand and began walking her a little faster through the surf, not slowing down until the dogs had ceased their barking.

They were about two hundred and fifty metres to the east of Casa al-Riyadh. They had been passing, fronting the beach, a network of narrow roads laid down a quarter of a century before as the start to an urbanization which had never got any further off the ground. The asphalt was full of holes, crumbling, sagging here, bulging there, the streetlights were rusted and broken. As Forbes and Leila left the beach and began to make their way across this sad area Forbes took a look at the arms dealer's house through his binoculars; it appeared much the same from this side as the other: only the tower in view, the double chain-link fence, close-packed cypress trees beyond it.

An ill-kept public road linked into the urbanization roads and meandered past the front of Casa al-Riyadh for several hundred metres to the highway. At the front of the house there was no dog run; there was a cypress hedge in front of high railings into which were let a pair of massive gates. They were made of bronze with a three-metre-high design incorporating an elephant on each one; the elephants were facing one another, their tusks almost meeting. On each of the top corners of the gates lurked a security camera.

'No elephants in Saudi,' commented Forbes as they strolled past.

'At least they're African and not Indian. Look at the size of their ears.'

Forbes suddenly leant his face close to Leila's as if to kiss her. 'Ssssh!' he hissed. He hurried her on towards the far end of the hedge.

'Why did you shush me?' she asked quietly as he slowed them down.

'Not only the elephants have ears. The cameras, too. Highly sensitive ones. I should have noticed right away. Christ, I'm slipping. Something like that could cost me my life.'

'We didn't say anything dangerous, did we?'

'I don't think so. I mentioned Saudi, but then the house name al-Riyadh's on the gates.'

They had almost reached the end of the hedge when there was a slight squeak behind them; the gates began to open. Forbes took hold of his Nikon.

'Up against the cypress,' he told Leila. 'We're taking holiday snaps again. Pose. Something a bit zany.' Angling her on the corner where cypress met dog run, he got himself in front of her so that the pictures would have the road towards the gates in the background. She stood on one leg, hooking the other up behind her and waved two arms in the air, flapper style, as if doing the Charleston.

A silver-grey stretch Cadillac Fleetwood Brougham with darkened windows, seven metres long, nosed out into the narrow road. Following it was a red Mercedes 280 SL and finally a black Mercedes 600 limousine. As the impressive little procession approached them Forbes snapped away while Leila struck various silly poses, laughing and poking her tongue out. He was getting very clear shots of the cars in the background; Leila was out of focus.

The twelve-wheeled show of money rolled past them. Then it stopped. The rear doors of the big Merc were flung open. Two ominously large, shirt-sleeved men with bulges beneath the sides of their shirts, got out and hurried towards Forbes and Leila. A third man, equally bulky, stuck a foot out on to the asphalt and watched.

They were about the same size as Forbes himself, but swarthy-faced, unpretty. One held out a meaty hand. 'The film,' he said.

Forbes found himself obliged to act the indignant moron. 'Now, just a *minute*, they're our holiday snaps,' he protested.

As she marched angrily to his side, Leila was

thinking: enraged little wifey. 'You leave him alone, you bullies,' she told them.

'Do be quiet, my love,' Forbes said in a contrived, upper-class accent. 'I can handle this. Now listen, my good fellow, you can't just go around demanding people's film. It's not on.'

A hairy fist closed around his Nikon. With his unarmed combat training – Forbes was an expert, as dangerous as a karate black belt – he could have taken them both on and laid them flat in the road. But there were other men in the cars, and they were armed. Besides, to attack would be utterly counter-productive; he was the dumb, innocent tourist. Nevertheless, restraint took a certain amount of will-power.

'Our boss, he a Muslim, see?' said the man who was tugging Forbes's camera. 'You most likely got a photo of him in that. He very religious man. He believe the camera, it steal his spirit.'

'But they are pictures of my *wife*. You can't *do* this, you know, you . . .'

He put up a totally ineffectual struggle as one heavy pinned his arms and the other opened the camera, removed the film, unrolled it completely and tossed it into the field at the edge of the road.

'Don't take no more pictures around here, mister.'

'But this is Spain, not darkest Africa. We're in the Common Market here. We . . .'

They were already clambering into their car. The man who had exposed the film threw over his shoulder: 'So why don't you complain to the Guardia Civil?'

The doors slammed and they were gone, the little motorcade accelerating around a corner and going almost out of sight as it sped through a pine wood.

'That really pissed me off,' Forbes snarled. 'I wanted to take the bastards and I didn't dare.'

Leila giggled. 'We're in the Common Market here,' she said, imitating his put-on accent. 'Prize, *prize*!'

His eyes followed them as, a hundred metres distant, the cars shot out of the wood to its right and neared the main road.

'Bingo,' he said.

'What bingo? You lost the bloody film.'

'Unimportant. The driver of the little red Merc, man in a round, flat, brimless hat? That was no less a personage than Sheikh Sulman himself.'

'You're sure? He drives his own car?'

'It was him all right. So. He likes to drive, does he? And he doesn't stay bottled up in his own world all the time. That's probably going to make our job so much easier.' He gripped Leila's hand hard. He was all tensed up within; the excitement of the game was seething through him, activating his libido. 'You know how I feel, don't you?' he asked her, eyes piercing hers as he squeezed her tiny hand.

She knew all right. She was only too familiar with that burning look. It had the identical sexual effect on her as his excitement had had upon him.

'A quickie,' she muttered. 'You want a quickie, you horny bastard. Where?'

He nodded towards the wood. 'There.'

The floor of the wood was prettily dotted with blue-leaved wild lilacs and spread with pine cones. Here and there, irritatingly, was the typical product of the Spanish family Sunday picnic – rubbish. In no place was this copse dense, but towards its sunlight-dappled centre there was an area where the roads were only vaguely glimpsed through the trees. Here there were some gorse thickets with dainty yellow flowers and with sharp spines instead of leaves; in among them, an incongruous intruder in what was mainly a pine wood, stood a knotty carob tree.

Forbes, mind and body intent on one thing only, muscular belly filled with nervous anticipation, led Leila by the hand towards the tree. She was treading carefully, eyes to the ground, taking no chances with her bare feet; tough they might be, but tougher still were the little stones and occasional pieces of broken glass which lay in ambush beneath the pine needles.

The carob was on a small, grassy hump, exposed parts of its roots clinging to the ground like thick, black, gnarled fingers. Pausing beneath its twisted branches, Forbes unhooked his camera and binoculars from his neck and put them on the ground together with his towel and his ridiculous Costa del Sol hat.

'But there's no place to lie down,' muttered Leila, pulse racing.

'Who said anything about lying down?'

Taking her by the armpits, he lifted her on to the hump of the tree to plant her crimson-nailed feet among the dead leaves and black, edible, chocolate-flavoured pods which had fallen from its branches. Her face was level with his. Their mouths hungrily meshed together, their tongues mingled. He pressed his groin into her and she gasped into his mouth. He was hard – he had been ever since first entering the wood. He lifted her a little higher so that their loins met and rubbed himself against her. Then he broke the kiss and backed slightly off her.

'Feel me.'

Weak with need for him, she reached between his legs to fondle him.

'Take my trunks down.'

She obliged, the faintest tremble in her hands. His erection, good and sturdy, sprang into view. Leaving his shorts crumpled above his knees she took hold of him, fisting, gently rubbing. He could drive her insane with need, this virile man of hers. After two years of marriage he still made love to her more frequently out of bed than in it; often in intriguing places like this wood where there was the chance, however slight, of being caught at it.

'Turn around.' Harsh. Urgent.

She faced the tree. He backed her off it and bent her into it. Her hands gripped the knobbly trunk. Then he dragged her bikini bottom down to the same area on her smooth and shapely legs as his shorts occupied on his and with no further preamble rammed his penis all the way inside her. Her ecstatic shout disturbed a flock of sparrows and they flew twittering from the highest branches.

It was destined to be a short but powerful coupling. As he steadily rocked his hips, Forbes fumbled undone the catch of her top and with it hanging loose from her shoulders he cupped both her delightful breasts in his hands and fondled them.

Through the trees, she was aware of the main road, a hundred and fifty metres or so distant, and its constant stream of traffic. The idea of all those people speeding by, and the thought that if a car happened to stop and the occupants were to take a close look into the copse they would see what was happening, added to Leila's lubricity. Orgasm began to clutch her in a hot, feverish grip.

This was no occasion for controlled, sustained lovemaking. He had been almost overcome with his need. With a massive grunt of thankful release, Forbes flooded into his woman – his only woman, the only one he ever wanted – while she whimpered through a string of small climaxes, then wailed the big one into the trees and at the highway.

'God,' mumbled Leila, minutes later, limp and drained and happy as, swimwear properly arranged over the places it was designed to cover, they left the carob and began to pick their way out of the wood. 'That was sooo . . .' She shook her head.

'It was, it was.' Forbes squeezed her hand. He was thoroughly replete, perfectly relaxed.

As they again enraged the Rottweilers by strolling down the western edge of the garden towards the beach, he cast a speculative eye through the heavy wire fence of the dog run. The slope up to Casa al-Riyadh from that side of the house was far gentler than the other. Trees and bushes, many of the bushes dense rhododendrons with showy clusters of pink and white flowers, abounded on the superbly tailored lawns but still afforded occasional glimpses of the villa between them. In a clumsy sort of hacienda style, it was enormous, with antique-yellow-washed walls. The windows were heavily barred.

'We're going to have to pay them a night visit,' said Forbes. They had reached the beach and the frantic barking of the dogs was dying down. 'I need to run a test on their after-dark security.'

'No time like tonight, boss,' chirped Leila. She pulled her hand from his, skipped down to the water's edge and began splashing her way back in the direction of the dunes where their funny little purple car was parked. She was feeling especially girlish and rather naughty after their open-air lovemaking. She stopped and waited for him, up to her knees in the surging sea. 'Let's join these wicked people and enjoy an hour or so's nude sunbathing,' she suggested when he caught her up.

'You bet.' He dropped his trunks.

A dark, squinting eye narrowed at the viewing end of the high-powered telescope in the turret of Casa al-Riyadh. Arab loins twitched hungrily. Leila, her image clear and almost close enough to reach out and touch, had stripped off her bikini.

'They're bare-arsed again,' the man said in Saudi Arabic to his companion as he watched Forbes and Leila link hands and begin walking through the surf away from them. 'The chick's got a gorgeous butt.'

'So don't hog it all to yourself.'

The second Arab took the telescope as Forbes and Leila left the sea, found a patch of sand to their liking and lay down. 'They set the dogs off twice,' he grunted. 'They were taking photos outside the house. You don't think that . . . ?'

'Nah. Not a chance. Just a couple of nutty tourists.'

'What I couldn't do for that baby doll. She doesn't know what she's missing!'

4

The summer tourist rush was not yet properly under way. That would start at the beginning of July. Forbes and Leila had no trouble getting a late dinner in the Green Pepper Greek restaurant at Marbella's famous Puerto Banús. Afterwards they lingered over drinks in the Playback. Such was Marbella night-life that the club was only just beginning to fill when they left at a little after two.

The night was bright with stars, but there was only a nail-paring of moon. Compared with during the day, there was very little traffic on the N340. The highway was divided in the middle with a concrete, concave-curved crash barrier – rather garishly painted with blue and white stripes through the municipality of Marbella – and Leila was obliged to drive a kilometre and a half past Sulman's villa before reaching an underpass to take them on to his side of the road.

'Kill the lights,' Forbes said as, still on the

highway, they approached the area of the pine wood. He was dressed all in black, wearing a thin cotton T-shirt, jeans and trainers.

They arrived at the turn-off which led to the little road through the copse. The tall cypress hedge and the illuminated front gates of Casa al-Riyadh were clearly visible in the distance for a few seconds, then Forbes told Leila to turn the Twingo into the copse.

'There's a flat area just down here on the left where you can park among the trees,' he said, eyes straining in the dark; what he wouldn't have given for night-vision goggles at that moment.

'I could put the lights on for a moment. We're hidden from the house.'

'No. The trees aren't that dense. The slightest flash will show up on their cameras.'

'OK.'

'I think we're coming to it now. Let's hope there's no one having it off in a car in there.'

There were no lovers – and there was just enough light from the stars to enable Leila, with the very greatest of care, to manoeuvre the little car in among the pines without doing it any damage.

'Here.'

She parked and switched off the engine. There was not a breath of wind. It was utterly still, quiet and warm. Forbes got out and went around to the back, pine needles softly scrunching beneath his rubber composition soles. He took a long, narrow box from the boot and then sat down in his seat with it across his lap, leaving his door open. There was no light in the car, since he had switched off the automatic interior bulb activator when they left the port; he had been pleased about that, for it meant his brain was in top gear.

In near darkness, he opened the box across his and Leila's thighs. Inside, its components housed in neat, fawn baize slots, was an L96A1 sniper rifle, a silencer, a Schmidt and Bender night-vision telescopic sight and some 7.62mm ammunition.

'I thought that's what it had to be, but you didn't answer when I asked you,' said Leila.

'I don't like talking about guns.' Forbes took the pieces one by one from the box and fitted them into place. 'It's bad luck.' He grinned in the dark. 'I just like using them.'

'I thought we were supposed to bring the sheikh in with his boots on, not bump him off,' Leila joked. She needed a joke. The sight of the rifle under her nose had tightened her nerves right up. It brought back vivid memories of her terrorist days.

'His boots will be on.'

'Where did you get it? We didn't bring it through customs, did we?'

'Yes we did. I had it tucked up my . . .' He laughed softly. 'Amazingly, our accountant pest produced it. He got it from the Kuwaiti embassy in Madrid. Useful places, embassies.'

Somewhere nearby an owl hooted; there was a rustle in some gorse which may have been its field mouse quarry. From his pocket Forbes produced a pair of thin black cotton gloves and pulled them on. He rolled a black cotton hood down over his face; only his eyes and his slightly wonky nose showed through.

Leila shivered. 'Should I feel safe with you?'

'No.' His voice was muffled by the mask. 'Sit tight. If you hear me shout, be ready to get the hell out of here. Otherwise stay very still and quiet, whatever happens. OK?'

'Do I get paid for this?'

'I paid you. Right here in this very wood. This morning. Or had you forgotten?' He rubbed his nose on hers, then he was gone, ducking low, slipping carefully through the trees in the direction of Casa al-Riyadh.

When he got to the edge of the wood he picked a spot where there was some longish grass, dropped down flat on his belly among it and wriggled forward on his elbows, rifle flat in front of him in both hands, making his cautious way towards a clump of gorse. Once he was there he slotted a soft-nosed, 7.62mm bullet into the breech of the rifle and arranged himself in a comfortable firing position, the adjustable rubber butt pad resting against his shoulder. Through the telescopic lens he carefully examined each of the security cameras over the elephant gates. They had identical wide-angle lenses, the one on the left presenting a better target since it was pointed almost directly towards him.

Very carefully, Forbes aligned the cross-hairs of the sight until they were in the dead centre of the camera lens. He took a deep breath, held it in and, exactly as he had first been trained almost thirty years before, slowly squeezed the trigger. There was a faint plop. At what seemed exactly the same moment as the rifle's recoil slammed his shoulder, the security camera lens exploded.

He lay there, very still on his belly, aware of his pulse, as he waited for the reaction. Two things happened in quick succession. The first was what he had more or less expected; the second was utterly unpredictable. Alarm sirens went off and the house was suddenly lit in a blaze of floodlights as bright as day as the Rottweilers woke up and went berserk. At the same time, a dark-coloured Citroën saloon, headlights on full beam, shot out of the road through the wood and came to an erratic, squealing stop near the house gates. Leaving the engine running, the driver opened his door. Clearly very much the worse for drinking, he lurched from the car, hands at his fly, desperate to empty his bladder.

A smaller gate in one of the elephants slammed open. First one armed man, then another, then yet another spilled into the road. As Forbes, unmoving except to carefully slip a clip of regular, 7.62mm ammunition into his sniper rifle, watched, they blew out the lights of the Citroën, which were glaring directly at them. The drunk made the fatal error of bringing his hands in shock up from his fly, one of them clumsily riding up under his jacket.

The heavies asked no questions. Without hesitation, they gunned him down. His body fell twitching to the dusty road, blood pouring from five wounds.

Four more armed men erupted from the gate. As two hauled the dead man into his car, the other five began hunting around in the immediate vicinity. Forbes was a good shot and a fast shot and he was equipped with a first-class rifle. Should he be spotted he would take most of them out before they got him; with luck he'd take all of them.

Apart from his eyes, which he slitted almost closed, he was entirely black and, buried in the sharp black shadows of the bush thrown by the floodlights, invisible. One man came close enough to almost stop Forbes's heart, then he turned his back.

The main gates were opened just enough for the Citroën with its slain drunk to be driven through. They closed. The floodlights stayed on.

As one by one the heavies disappeared through the belly of the elephant Forbes began to perform the uncomfortable stunt of crawling backwards on his stomach to the wood, rifle ever ready for action. Once within the shelter of the trees, where the floodlights afforded him plenty of deep shadow cover, he straightened up and hurried back to Leila and the Twingo.

He could almost feel her fear; it seemed to be hanging around in the air. 'Christ, Stephen,' she muttered, 'what the bloody hell? I was terrified for you.'

'Good kid for staying quiet. Starting the car, a show of lights, could have got us both killed.' He clambered into the Twingo and stripped off his gloves and hood.

'What was happening?'

He told her, finishing: 'I only wanted to test their reaction. Jesus, they reacted. The poor drunken bastard chose that moment to stop and take a leak. It was unbelievable.'

'But the security camera, Stephen. Won't they know it was shot out? Won't that put them on their guard?'

'I doubt they'll find any trace of a bullet, even supposing they look. It was soft-nosed, it would have flattened and disintegrated on impact. They'll come to the conclusion there was some sort of a fault in the glass and, like spotlights often do, it exploded. In any case, why would somebody intent on raiding the house not follow it through? Why kill just one camera then vanish?'

'And the poor bastard?'

'They'll check him out, realize their mistake and bury him.' He was still completely keyed up. His eyes roved hungrily over her. 'You know what I'd like to do? Right here and now?'

'Uh-uh. No you *don't*.' She shoved his skirt-invading hand away and started the engine. 'I'm getting us out of here while we're still breathing.'

'Shit. OK, but no lights,' he cautioned. 'Nice and easy.' He leant towards her to kiss the softness of her neck, just below her ear. 'I'll keep it on ice until we get home.'

5

With a telephone receiver jammed between his shoulder and his ear, Forbes was scribbling notes on a Marbella Club memo pad. 'I'll ring you back in a little while to confirm all this,' he said. 'Meanwhile, make a provisional booking for midday.' He hung up.

Leila, wearing a neat, crimson miniskirt and a black silk blouse with ruffles, was folded into an armchair, her legs tucked up under her. She was leafing through the spring edition of a glossy magazine called *Marbella Life*. With its cover picture of the head and shoulders of a beautiful woman it looked like a woman's monthly, but it wasn't – it was a quarterly featuring news and views from the area, and society pages.

Seconds after Leila said: 'Heh, what do you know, babes, here's our sheikh,' the bungalow doorbell chimed.

It was Hammid Mullah, overdressed for the sunshine coast, every inch the accountant in his dark-grey pinstripe suit, pale-blue shirt and quiet, formal tie.

'Good timing,' Forbes told him, thinking: arsehole. 'Here.' He handed him his scribbled memo sheet. It was the cost of the hire of a four-seater light aircraft with pilot for two hours together with a competent photographer.

Mullah briefly scanned the note. His eyes wandered to Forbes's Nikon, which was sitting uncased on a coffee table. 'Can't you take the pictures?' he asked it.

Forbes gave him a blank look as he struggled to disguise his dislike of the man. 'Sure I could,' he said. 'But I'm no pro. If I cock up the relevant pictures it's going to cost you the plane a second time.'

The accountant sighed heavily. He shook his head. His tired gaze lifted to the wooden-beamed ceiling. 'Approved.'

As he left, Forbes was punching the numbers of the Málaga plane hire company on his phone. 'What a character,' he grunted. 'Approved! He even initialled my fucking note!'

Leila frowned. 'I do wish you'd reserve that word for bed.'

'You're just a little crazy, you know that?' He grinned at her, then spoke into the telephone, confirming his bookings. That done, he said:

'What was that you said a while back about the sheikh?'

'Here.' Leila uncurled her bare feet from under her; the nails were painted bright green. She walked over to him with the opened magazine and pointed out a small black and white photograph on a page of ten.

'So,' he said. 'Little Yasser's a social butterfly.'

'Little?'

'He's not very tall. Five-nine. He wears girls-love-tall-men shoes.' He studied the photographs with great interest. They were of a New Year's Eve party thrown by the American one-time owner of Avon Cosmetics, the Baroness Terry von Pantz, the title from her deceased Austrian husband. Almost all the guests at the black-tie affair who were depicted in the magazine had titles; there was Prince Ferdinand von Bismarck, the Marqués de Cortina and the Duc d'Uzès, among other notables. And there was the Scottish film star James Kennedy, affecting a black T-shirt beneath his dinner jacket. Sheikh Sulman, in one of his funny little round, flat hats – a silver-sequinned one presumably meant to suit the occasion – was sitting with the Honourable Alexandra Foley on one side of him and a well-known Hollywood actor's widow on the other. There was no doubt it was him – his name was beneath the photo.

'Illustrious company.' Forbes tossed the magazine on to a coffee table. 'It seems to be very well established that our friend Yasser doesn't lock himself away in his Shangri-La. Good news.'

'Sheikh, rattle and roll,' said Leila, brightly.

He laughed.

She picked up *Marbella Life*, glancing again at the page of New Year photos. 'The do was at the Olivia Valère nightclub in Puente Romano,' she observed. 'Right next door to here. I think it's the old Régine's.'

'And you bet your sweet life he had two carloads of goons sitting outside all night.' He got to his feet. 'Time we were on our way.'

She glanced disapprovingly at him. 'We're supposed to be in the real estate business today, remember? I don't think jeans and a denim shirt quite fit the part.'

'What would I do without you?'

'Some other lucky chick.'

It was another very warm day. In that area of the world it was common for businessmen, and even politicians, to go without ties and jackets. Forbes changed into yellow cotton trousers, white shoes and a white, open-necked, silk shirt.

They arrived at Málaga's Club Aeronáutico — a flying club attached to the airport — at precisely twelve o'clock to find a twenty-year-old twin-engined Comanche awaiting them. Leila climbed up beside the pilot, and Forbes, carrying detailed maps of the Marbella and Estepona districts, went in the back with the photographer. On the maps he had red-ringed twenty houses; nineteen were of no interest to him whatsoever, but they were his cover, his excuse for having aerial shots taken of Casa al-Riyadh.

Marbella from the air, with its impressive backdrop of the majestic mountain known as La Concha – The Shell – its surroundings of luxury villas with beautiful gardens, presented an appearance about as close to an earthly Paradise as one could get. Its brand-new appearance had been developed over the previous three years by perhaps the punchiest mayor in the history of Spain, Jesús Gil y Gil. It abounded in perfectly tended parks, public gardens and fountains. As it traversed the town, the highway was bounded on both sides by flower-beds, and the fancy brickwork central barriers were choked with flowers. For all of the ten kilometres from Marbella to the next town, San Pedro de Alcantara, and beyond, the flowers and plants continued; even the many flyover bridges had immaculately gardened banks.

Forbes had had the photographer dig out his most powerful telephoto lens; he wanted sharp, clear, close-up shots without the necessity of going in too low and disturbing the occupants of Casa al-Riyadh.

They took pictures of eleven houses before overflying the sheikh's Estepona retreat. It was vast and sprawling. There were two swimming pools: a large one in an inner patio and an Olympic-sized one in front of the house. There was an ornamental lake with a small island and a bridge going to it. There were three tennis courts. On the white-paved drive there was room for fifty cars. And there was a helicopter pad with a twin-engined Chinook Mark II sitting at rest on it.

From a height of five hundred metres the photographer rapidly shot half a roll of film as they cruised over Casa al-Riyadh in one direction, then used up the rest as they circled and went off in the other.

They were peeling off towards the mountains when Forbes's eyes were attracted by traffic movements down below; the same little motorcade as the morning before was leaving the house.

He very much wanted to find out where they were off to; on the other hand he could not betray this interest to the pilot and photographer. The N340 was in view below them for several kilometres in either direction. The convoy — the silver-grey stretch Cadillac in front, the bright-red Mercedes 280SL in the middle and the black Merc 600 behind – was easy to keep track of provided the Comanche did not stray too far from the road. Forbes asked the pilot to keep on the sea side and get well in front of the sheikh. Searching his map he found a large house he had not ringed, on the Guadalmina golf estate. He had the pilot slow to the plane's lowest cruising speed and circle that house and the photographer take pictures until the sheikh's procession was well ahead of them and entering the San Pedro crossroads. He then got the pilot to follow the road again at moderate speed, slowly overhauling the fast-moving convoy.

Halfway between San Pedro and Marbella the sheikh turned off towards the foothills on the road to the mountain village of Istán, passing close by where King Fahd, the monarch of his country, kept a holiday palace fashioned on the style of the American White House. The cars continued for a kilometre or so before turning into the rhododendron-lined drive of a large and stately home.

Forbes's instinct was to take a couple of shots of this house, but his judgement warned him against it; he had taken risks enough of arousing the sheikh's suspicions for one day. He ringed the property in blue on his map and ordered the pilot on his way, to get the task of having pictures taken, in which he had no interest, finished.

Sheikh Sulman switched off the engine of the smaller Mercedes, leant forward over his steering wheel, staring into the bright blue sky with a frown on his face, his eyes following the white Comanche until it disappeared from sight. His thin, brown hand was clutching the knee of his young woman passenger. She was nineteen, plumpish, exactly the way he loved them, the latest in a series of 'hostesses' sought out for him by a man in his permanent employ to do simply that; a man paid also to ensure before each girl was employed that she would acquiesce to his master's deviant sexual demands, for Sulman was an occasional pederast who enjoyed, among other somewhat kinky habits, performing with girls the same act that he did with young men.

Forbes's plane bothered the sheikh. It had been brought to his attention that it had circled and overflown his villa twice, and now it had droned over the house he was visiting. By itself, he would have taken little notice of the event. But yesterday there had been that business of the irritating couple and the photographs and last night the strange affair of one of his security cameras shattering – plus the nuisance of the killed man, who it seemed had been nothing more threatening than a Spanish drunk. Trivial incidents, perhaps. Even the murder bothered him not in the slightest; he was, after all, a dealer in death on the grandest of scales. Trivial, yet taken together they niggled his instinct for survival.

He did not confide in the girl. He never revealed any of his innermost thoughts to paid women. A bodyguard let him out of his car, bowing his shaven head in the deferential manner upon which Sulman insisted.

Within the miniature manor house, Sophronia, Lady Sandhurst, tall and stately like the house itself, was peeping from behind a net curtain at her driveway. 'Oh God,' she said to her much shorter, thickset husband Charles, who was sipping his favourite tipple of Stolichnaya vodka on the rocks in their very British, slightly faded drawing room while scanning the *Financial Times*, 'the bloody man seems to have brought an army with him.'

'Shouldn't surprise you, my love,' said Lord Sandhurst, mildly. 'You've been told he never visits anywhere without his bodyguards. You've even seen it at Terry's.'

'Yes, but . . . I didn't *dream* he'd . . . I mean, *here*, dammit! Villa Fuchsia happens to be a most respectable house.'

He peered at her over his reading glasses, an

enigmatic twinkle in his eye. 'Does it now? I can think of a thing or two . . .'

'Yes, well, never *mind*, Charles.'

While flattered to have her invitation accepted by this almost legendary Arab with his rumoured billions and his DC1O, 747 and helicopter, she found herself upset, a little unnerved even, at his show of strength on her private property. She had organized a small lunch party for him, inviting three other couples who had yet to show up. Apart from anything else she was scared that the ugly characters littering her drive would frighten them away.

'I hope he doesn't expect me to feed that bunch of hoodlums,' she said.

Lord Sandhurst jointed his wife behind the curtain as Sulman, straightening his red silk hat, a hand on his companion's chubby, bare elbow, began to walk her up the short flight of tiled steps to the double front doors.

'Of course he doesn't, cherub,' he opined. 'They're bound to have lunch-boxes.' He smoothed his grey moustache as his lively eyes twinkled on the girl. 'But we'll have to feed *her*.' He cleared his throat. 'Not bad at all. Peaches and cream, what?'

She glared at him. 'Peaches and *what*? You're a nitwit, Charles, and your taste is abominable. Can't you tell a bloody tart when she's dangled under your nose?'

The old brass ship's bell by the side of the antique wooden front doors pealed loudly twice as Sheikh Yasser Sulman tugged on its rope.

At five o'clock that afternoon the forecourt of Da Paulo's swanky café in Puerto Banús was almost full. At three of the tables people were engrossed in games of backgammon. Hand in hand, Forbes and Leila strolled along the quay-side from nearby Antonio's restaurant, where they had just finished a late and expensive lunch. They found an empty table at Da Paulo's and ordered coffee.

This corner of the port was one of the most idyllic of spots in which to while away an hour or two on a sunny afternoon. Medium-sized yachts were anchored before it on either side of a quay which stretched at right angles a hundred metres into the harbour from where Forbes and Leila had parked their backsides. The boats were bobbing slightly as a rising, friendly breeze ruffled the water; their pennants were tinkling and flapping. People of mixed ages, nationalities and social classes wandered idly up and down, a far higher proportion of them elegantly dressed and well off than would be found in an average crowd. The general atmosphere, as ever in this sybaritic place, was one of relaxed good humour.

Forbes, too, was in good spirits. The photographic expedition, he felt, had been most worthwhile. He had taken the unexposed rolls of film from the photographer and sent the one with the shots of Casa al-Riyadh — he had been most careful to mark it — by jet service to the Kuwaiti Embassy in London, where they would be developed and blown up to the maximum usable size, section by section. He was convinced that they would tell him a great deal more about the house and its security than he already knew, and that if there was a weak spot in its defences it would show up. And there had been the unexpected bonus of pinpointing a villa belonging to one of Sulman's friends.

'Why so broody, chicken?' Leila asked him as she stirred her coffee.

'Reviewing the situation, as they say. We seem to be making progress.'

'Hope so. We need the rest of that half a million.'

He smiled at her, then said pleasantly: 'Mercenary little bitch.'

'Not half. With a mercenary husband. A real one.'

Over on a corner by the side of Antonio's restaurant a pair of skinny girls were modelling for a fashion photographer. 'Oh, for a nice quiet life like theirs,' said Leila.

He followed her eyes. 'You'd get bored.'

'Maybe.'

He poured a little anis into his coffee and drank some. As he glanced around at the other tables, studying the occupants of each one, he said: 'Well, kid, we now have a clearer idea of what we're up against and it's not exactly going to be taking candy from a baby. Next step is to organize full-time surveillance on sheikhy boy.'

'Just you and me, still?'

'You got it. That is, until I've worked out a way of just how . . . and where . . .' His words tailed off. He was staring across the crowded forecourt, eyes narrowing.

'What's up?' asked Leila.

'The arsehole who wrecked my film yesterday. One of the three who blew away the poor bastard last night.'

'He's here?'

'I'm looking right at him. He's playing back-gammon. There are just two tables between us.'

Leila knocked her coffee spoon on the floor and took a peek at the man while picking it up. 'It's him all right.'

Forbes's face had tensed; his jawbone had set in the way it did when he was burning with anger. 'I can forgive him the film but not that poor bastard.'

'But he's not the object of the exercise, lover.'

'The exercise just took a temporary change in direction.'

She did not much care for his change in expression. Personal hostility was hardly going to contribute to the cause. She put a hand over his, a fingertip resting on his slim gold Vacheron Constantin watch. 'Forget it, Stephen,' she pleaded. 'You're going to complicate things.' But the stupid sod won't, she thought. The anger bug's bit him.

He smiled grimly at her. 'I'm going to complicate *him*.' A smart, white-jacketed waiter was at the heavy's table, bowing and scraping as he took an order. 'The fucking waiter's licking his arse.'

Leila decided on flippancy. She knew her man too well; no way was she going to dissuade him from dishing out his brand of justice. 'It's a dirty job, but somebody's got to do it,' she said, watching the waiter.

Forbes waited patiently for his moment – if indeed there was going to be such a moment. Leila was unhappy about the situation but not unduly worried; whatever Stephen decided to do to the man she knew it would be done professionally.

Some half an hour later there was a shout of disgust from the backgammon player in question. He banged his dice cup down on to the board hard enough for the sound to be heard all over the forecourt and to make the pieces jump; his opponent had evidently rolled a freakily lucky combination. Springing to his feet, the heavy hurried into the bar.

'Maybe losing makes him need a pee,' Forbes observed. He poured the cold dregs from his coffee cup into the saucer. Clutching the cup in his right hand he got up. 'I'm going to make him wet his pants.' Taking his time, he went off in the same direction as his new target.

The décor within Da Paulo's was thirties style, with light-brown veneered woodwork, figurine lamps and two walls full of mirrors with hand-painted designs around their edges. At the far end of the bar was an open, carpeted staircase leading to the toilets; the man was just disappearing at its top.

Clutching the sturdy little coffee cup hard in his fist, Forbes followed him up.

The gentlemen's loo was small. There was a hand basin and mirror and beyond it a door behind which was the toilet itself. The outer door did not lock, the inner did. But the Arab was peeing and he had not bothered to fully close the inner door. Forbes went in, closing the outer door, and waited quietly, his adrenalin rising.

When the Arab zipped himself up and moved out to wash his hands, Forbes made room for him; there was barely enough space for two big men. He placed a hand on the knob of the inner door. The man gave him no more than a cursory glance; in any case it was unlikely he would identify this smooth-looking character with the grockle in luminous yellow-framed sunglasses and a stupid hat of the day before.

As the Arab turned on a tap and sluiced his hands, Forbes said softly: 'Do you remember a movie called *The Hustler*?'

The heavy glanced sharply up at Forbes's reflection in the mirror, a question on his lips which would never be asked. The tough little coffee cup, held like a rock in the Englishman's powerful fist, cracked into the man's temporal bone, just below his left ear. Making no sound beyond a soft grunt, he slumped forward, unconscious, over the sink and slipped to the floor, crumpling through the inner door.

'In that pretty picture,' muttered Forbes, grimly enjoying himself, 'Paul Newman got both his thumbs broken – curiously enough, in a loo.'

Which is exactly what, quickly and efficiently, he did. Taking hold of the Arab's right hand, he bunched his fingers together and ripped the thumb backwards against the base joint. It was torn out of its socket with a sound like a snapping twig and immediately began to swell. Pulling the other arm from beneath the man, he did the same thing to the left thumb. Without another look he left the toilet and hurried down the stairs. A man on the way up took no notice of him.

'On your feet, love,' he said to Leila as he reached their table and there was a muffled shout from within the bar. 'It might be wise to make ourselves scarce.'

As he walked Leila slowly away and down an alley through the semi-rustic port buildings, he said, immense satisfaction in his voice: 'Son of a bitch won't be shooting people in the foreseeable future. Or ruining their film.' He grinned, draping an arm over Leila's shoulder. 'He won't be shaking dice for a while, either.'

'He ought to thank you,' said Leila. 'You've probably saved him a bundle.'

6

It was late morning, two days later. Forbes and Leila were taking a little sun. They were stretched out side by side on loungers at the Marbella Beach Club close to the big pool, whose filtration system took the water through an impressive cascade.

The detailed aerial photographs of Casa al-Riyadh had arrived earlier from the Kuwaiti Embassy in London via jet service, and Forbes had pored over them on the bungalow terrace. The negatives had been blown up to such an extent that had the fifteen by twenty-centimetre prints taken from each one been put together the resulting pictures would have covered a double bed. Enlarged even to this extent, they were perfectly clear with only a slight tendency towards graininess. He was very satisfied with them. They pinpointed all the security cameras – there were fourteen – and the floodlights. The dog run did not continue behind the front cypress hedge – it occupied only three sides of the garden. But behind the hedge and its hidden iron railings there was a second, three-metre-high iron fence and there was a second pair of massive gates in this fence, ten metres beyond the first pair. What Forbes could not glean from the pictures was how much manpower there was within the house. It seemed to have about fifty bedrooms — enough accommodation for a small army.

Lying there quietly in the sunshine, eyes following two nubile young ladies who were taking a dip, Forbes gave every impression of the perfectly relaxed holidaymaker lazing away the hour before lunch. Actually his brain was in top gear, struggling with the problem which faced him. He realized that, short of getting inside the sheikh's fortress, he was unlikely to obtain any more information about it than he already had; he was more or less giving up the idea of taking the man out of his house — apart from with a full-scale commando-style attack it was virtually impregnable. While watching a blonde's bronzed breasts wobble delightfully as, water streaming off her, she heaved herself out of the pool, he was considering carefully all the knowledge they had gathered so far about the sheikh's movements beyond the house. He came to a conclusion.

'We're going to have to snatch him from his car,' he said, without turning his head towards Leila, his eyes on the blonde.

She blinked several times at him. 'Piece of cake.

Want me to do it on my tod, or were you planning to lend a hand?'

He failed to respond. 'We've watched him leave the house five times. Always the same story. The Cadi, him and a chick in the little red Merc, and four goons in the 600. But we don't know how many in the Cadi because of those damn black windows. There might just be two. There could be as many as eight, ten even. All tooled up, of course.'

'Maybe you'd better help me, after all.'

Forbes ignored his wife's banter. He spoke in the direction of the two lovelies who were plunging side by side into the pool to race each other across. 'He takes himself out a great deal, judging by what we've seen so far. Once each day, two nights. And he's given a small party. Those fifteen cars which showed up at his house last night were bringing local socialites, not Arabs. Nor particularly business people.'

The previous day he had found a part of the pine wood close to the highway where there were some gorse bushes from the cover of which there was a clear view, right through the trees, of the elephant gates. Just before ten in the evening, nightfall, despite her protests he had had Leila leave him there; he could do without an investigation of a parked Twingo. He had patiently watched the gates through his night-vision Leitz binoculars for hours, flat on his belly, getting more and more uncomfortable and stiffer and with only a hip-flask of Glenmorangie malt to comfort him.

When Leila showed up, at two-thirty per instructions and with the Twingo's lights off, the Glenmorangie had long since gone the way of all fine whisky once it leaves the shop, but Forbes's night of discomfort had had its reward, for he had recognized two of the faces in chauffeured cars as they left Casa al-Riyadh. Both had been in the photos of Baroness Terry von Pantz's New Year's bash in *Marbella Life*. One had been that of the baroness herself and the other the unmistakable countenance of superstar James Kennedy.

'I wish you'd stop ogling those birds,' grumbled Leila. 'You haven't taken your eyes off them.'

'As long as I keep my paws off.'

'Hah. Given half the chance you'd be bonking them.'

That made him look at her. He smiled. 'No I wouldn't.'

'I was just kidding.' Leaning across the little table with its bowl of fruit which divided the loungers, she planted a kiss among the forest of slightly greying hairs on his big chest. She had been thinking about Sulman, too. 'He's a fun guy, our little sheikh,' she said. 'Visiting all over the place, throwing parties. I wonder if all those important people would boogie with him if they knew the true nature of the beast? That he's an arms supplier to Saddam among others and not simply the multimillionaire international financier he describes himself as?'

'Sure they would. As long as someone down here's got bread, notoriety adds a little spice. Remember Khashoggi just before he went off to Switzerland to get nicked by Interpol and carted off to the Big Apple in handcuffs?'

She gave him a blank look.

'Of course, you wouldn't. Christ, time goes so bloody quickly it's terrifying. We hadn't even met. I was down here at the time. He . . .'

'With some other chick,' she interrupted.

'I was down here and he gave a great, glittering party in his mansion up in the hills somewhere. The pictures hit a couple of international magazines. All the Marbella jet set were there. Black tie. I bet most of the people who were at Yasser's last night were there. Yet no one in their right mind would think that Khashoggi was white as a new fall of snow.'

'No.' Leila watched the blonde as she walked with an exaggerated wiggle to her sunbed. 'She *has* got terrific tits.'

'I've got bored with them. I prefer yours.'

'Good. Sooo' – she drew the word out – 'we have a solution.'

'Yeah?'

'Sure. We gather together a bunch of your mercenary pals, we dress you and them up in penguin gear with shooters carefully concealed, you all gatecrash one of Sulman's parties and – jackpot. Half a million smackers.'

He laughed loudly. 'Penguin gear? Shooters? Smackers? I can tell you went to finishing school. Roedean was it, or in Switzerland?'

'Holloway.'

'If only it *were* that simple. Blast him out from the inside.'

'So how are you planning to grab him from his car?'

'Total surprise. Preferably at night. Seven crack men, including me.'

'What about little me?'

'No.'

'Come on. I'm good. I want to be there with you.'

'Shut it, doll. I'm not prepared to risk you.'

'But . . .'

'*No*, Leila.'

She sighed. 'OK. I know when I'm beaten.'

'We'll need some sort of a gimmick. Catch them totally off guard. I might need more brains than ours working on that. But before I start picking my men we should keep up another week's surveillance. See if there's any pattern at all to his movements – though I doubt if there will be. In the meantime we'll sniff out where some of his high society connections live. It may be gold dust.'

'Someone like this Baroness von something or other. She shouldn't be that difficult to track down.'

'Von Pantz. No.'

'She looked like a sweet lady from her photograph.'

'I'd be sweet with her sort of bread.'

'I bet she's one of the nicest women on the coast. I can tell. OK, what's next, mister?'

He sat up and pulled a shirt over his shoulders. 'We have a drink, we have lunch. I flirt with the . . .'

'You do *not* flirt with anybody.'

'I do not flirt with brown boobs. Then we go back to work.'

They watched the sheikh for a week, swapping the Twingo for a Fiesta and thereafter changing cars every day, Forbes hating it but forcing himself to spend four hours on six separate nights among gorse bushes on the far side of the wood from Casa al-Riyadh with his binoculars and Glenmorangie. Sulman's movements followed no obvious pattern, but he certainly moved, visiting almost every day and on three evenings, always sandwiched between two carloads of bodyguards in his Merc.

They discovered where four other friends of the sheikh lived – apart from Lord and Lady Sandhurst. Two of these four were the Baroness von Pantz and James Kennedy. Forbes noted that both of these huge houses, that of the baroness not far from Casa al-Riyadh itself and Kennedy's down on the beach near San Pedro at the end of a complicated, narrow confusion of ancient, tree-lined lanes, offered excellent prospects for setting up an ambush.

To the man on the Harley-Davidson who appeared on two evenings and once during the day, rounding the corner of the road coming from the abandoned urbanization to the west of the sheikh's villa and speeding up through the wood and then off down the highway, Forbes paid only the most cursory of attention.

That was a mistake which was to cost him dearly.

7

'Pissing down as usual. Nice to be back,' Forbes observed as he took a seat in front of Khalet Awadi's over-ornate desk. Rain was streaming so hard down the armour-plated glass of the embassy's casement windows that it was almost impossible to see out; here and there it was dribbling through the seventy-year-old wooden frames. 'I can't imagine why you choose to be in this country when you could be living in the sun.'

The Kuwaiti ambassador's dark eyes, as they studied him from behind his heavy-lensed spectacles, appeared larger than they were. He noted Forbes's golden suntan. 'We all have our cross to bear, Mr Forbes. Mine is the English weather.' He paused. 'What's yours?'

Forbes nearly quipped: a large Chivas on the rocks. Instead he said, though affably enough: 'Hammid Mullah.'

Awadi produced a genuine, non-diplomatic smile. 'I should have thought you'd have been able to deal with a mere accountant.'

'He quibbles. I detest quibblers.'

The ambassador shrugged the matter aside. 'Well?'

'I can take Sulman. It won't be exactly a pushover – his security's impressive. Why is the man so frightened? Does he know you're out to get him?'

'A leak's unlikely. This matter is between the ruler, the head of government, Mullah and yourself. But I imagine Sulman has a number of enemies.' He laughed flatly. 'Except for the fact that we'd make sure you wind up dead, you could probably sell him to the highest bidder once you got your hands on him.'

You actually have a sense of humour, Forbes thought. 'I'm not in the habit of crossing my employers.'

'One hopes not.' Awadi pounced on a cigarette which had been lying in wait on his desk in its silver holder and which he had been trying to resist. 'Also,' he said, lighting the Winston with a gold Dupont, 'I have evidence to make me believe the man's paranoiac. It would add to his sense of power to boast a show of strength.'

'His paranoia isn't a great deal of help to me.'

'But you assure me you can kidnap him. How many men will you need?'

'Six.' Forbes's eyes were dragged to a window

by the sudden noise of the violent pattering of rain; a summer storm was building up and the wind was beginning to gust, driving raindrops the size of hailstones hard against the glass. 'Flaming June,' he said.

'Quite. That would be six including you?'

'Excluding.'

'How much?'

'Each man will be a tried-and-tested expert in his field. A fighting machine. Utterly reliable, totally efficient. They don't come cheap and they'll be risking their lives. I can get them for twenty grand apiece.'

Awadi's lean jaw twitched. 'I'll have to clear it, of course, but in principle it's all right. We'll pay their flights and all expenses. Five thousand when they report for duty in Spain, the rest when you deliver Sulman.' He sucked on the ivory end of his cigarette-holder. 'Mullah will take care of it.'

'That's five grand apiece?'

'Yes.'

'Fine.' Forbes engaged the ambassador's eyes thoughtfully. 'Do you have anything resembling an air force in that country of yours?'

The question failed to amuse Awadi. 'We have rebuilt our air force, naturally. You think we want to continue to rely on the Americans?'

'I do believe we were in there somewhere as well,' Forbes remarked mildly. 'Anyhow, apart from the impossibility of getting their help to extradite Sulman, how's your diplomatic relationship with Spain?'

'Excellent.'

'Then it wouldn't present too much of a problem to get special clearance for a Kuwaiti Air Force plane to land at a Spanish airport if and when I need it?'

'Not at all. Depending of course on local air traffic.'

'It won't be a totally inflexible time.'

'Would you mind telling me . . . ?'

'With respect, yes I would,' Forbes cut in. His eyes flickered around the room. 'For all I know the embassy might be bugged. I'll let you know when it's closer to the event.'

'This embassy is swept regularly for bugs,' Awadi said coldly.

'I'm sure it is. When was the last time?'

The ambassador puffed irritably on his cigarette. 'Is there anything else you want, Mr Forbes?'

Forbes stood. 'Four hundred and sixty-seven grand,' he said, 'taking the fifty thousand dollars at one fifty. In money.'

8

'Making a living, Guy?'

The short, broad-shouldered man in the little electrical repair shop just off the Fulham Road glanced up in surprise from his workbench at the familiar voice, not heard for many years. His boyish face crumpled into a delighted grin. 'Stephen Forbes!' he exclaimed. 'As I live and breathe.'

'Hi, feller.' Forbes gave the man a friendly punch on the shoulder. He regretted not having brought an umbrella. Just hurrying from the double-parked taxi to the shop door had soaked his hair and turned the shoulders of his fawn raincoat a patchy dark brown. It was belting down, and thunder rumbled in the air. At ten past two in the afternoon, it was dark enough to be dusk.

'As I live and breathe,' repeated Guy Keegan. 'Courtesy of you. To be sure, I've never forgotten.'

'Shit, it was nothing.'

Keegan, born in the city of Cork thirty-five summers previously, climbed to his feet and pumped Forbes's hand enthusiastically. 'Same good-looking bastard,' he said as he studied him with a critical eye. 'Do I detect a sprinkling of silver in the thatch?'

'Grey, Guy. It's called grey. I thought about dying it but my wife insists it suits me.'

'So you have an old lady at home now, do you? Never thought you'd succumb, so I didn't.'

'She's twenty-six.'

'Figures. You always did have the luck of the Irish.'

'How's Betty?'

'Thirty-seven, more's the pity.'

'She's a wonderful lady.'

'She is that.' Keegan produced a bottle of Old Bushmills and two glasses from beneath his bench, set them down in front of Forbes and told him to help himself. He walked to the door, closed and locked it, and turned the sign around.

After splashing three fingers of the Irish whisky into a glass, Forbes glanced around the shop. It was crammed with a disorderly jumble of electrical appliances ranging from toasters and hair-driers to televisions, videos and CD players.

'How do you keep track of everything?' he asked Keegan as the man parked his behind on the bench next to him and poured himself a generous measure of whisky.

'I don't. But the punters sure as hell do.' He clinked glasses with Forbes.

'Cheers.'

'Cheers.'

'What was it you were wanting – your pacemaker fixed?'

Forbes laughed. He took a swig from his glass, not much liking the flavour of Old Bushmills but enjoying its raw heat as it hit his belly. 'I need an electronics expert who also happens to have a history as a reliable soldier of fortune.'

'That's seven years behind me, Steve, so it is. The mercenary stuff, I mean.'

'And now you're stuck in a little shop in Parsons Green tinkering around with busted whatsits.' Forbes stared flatly at him as Keegan knocked back a hefty slug of whisky. 'Hardly a job for the gutsy son of a bitch I once led in Nicaragua.'

'The gutsy SOB had enough after the gutshot, thanks a million.'

It had been near Matagalpa in 1987; a coup attempt in which Forbes had launched a surprise attack on a small detachment of the president's guard. But the surprise had been on them. It came in the form of a swooping helicopter, a black bird of death dropping on them out of the night with its searchlight eye and 7.62mm MI34 GECAL electric rotary Gatling gun for talons; six lethal talons which ripped flesh to pieces at some six thousand rounds per minute.

Sixteen of Forbes's nineteen good men had been shredded that fatal night. He himself had escaped with a thigh wound, managing by a combination of his legendary luck and the expert use of a Heckler & Koch rifle to put out the chopper's eye with a volley of 9mm Teflon-coated shells. With the guard post throwing out armed president's men like a sea of vomit, Forbes was hightailing it out of there in a jeep when he spotted movement among the carnage. As the other two survivors in the jeep let off everything they had against the guards, Forbes had turned back and rescued the wounded Irishman.

Downing his whisky, Forbes helped himself to two fingers more. He peered into the innards of the video Keegan had been repairing. 'What do you make in a day with this stuff, Guy?'

'Enough.'

'And to spare?'

'Does it matter?'

'Do with twenty big ones?'

'Who couldn't?'

'Why does an Irishman always answer a question with a question?'

'I could do with a little cash injection, to be

sure. But I'm kind of attached to my body arranged the way it is. I'm averse to it leaking, do you see?'

'Curiously enough, I suffer from the same reluctance.' Forbes was clicking the switch of a toaster on and off as he spoke. 'This one's a doddle, Guy. South of sunny Spain. One target with a handful of not over-bright bodyguards. No army, no jungle, no president, no . . .'

'Will you be leaving things alone, now?'

'What? Oh.' He pushed the toaster away from him. 'Five grand when you plant your bog-Irish boot on Spanish soil. Fifteen when we deliver a little man with a penchant for funny hats to the welcoming committee.'

Keegan swallowed his whisky nervously, Adam's apple bobbing, greyish eyes darting around his shop. Forbes recognized the signs. A hungry man. Temptation. 'One week, maybe two,' he said. 'You sleep in a bed in a nice, comfortable hotel, not some tent in the jungle. Twenty grand. You need it, Guy.'

'All right, fill me in.'

Next stop Little Venice, after a side trip to an umbrella shop. There seemed to be as much water pouring from the black sky into the canal as there was in it. The big, striped golf umbrella did not keep Forbes entirely dry. And he managed to plonk his foot into a torrent of gutter water as he stepped from the taxi.

Forbes descended a well-worn set of stone steps and followed the narrow towpath. Then, after passing several attractive houseboats bobbing gently in the downpour, he arrived at a converted barge abounding in colourfully painted pots and drowning flowers. Funny boat. Funnier name: *Nell Gwyn's Oranges*. He went aboard.

'Stripe me, if it ain't Steve McQueen!' exclaimed the balding man with the pugilist's face who, clad in a silk dressing-gown with a dragon belching fire on it, was watching tennis from Barcelona on a small television as Forbes descended into the gloom.

'Hi, Freddie,' Forbes said as he stood his half-closed brolly in a corner beneath the companionway. Water began immediately to puddle on the deck beneath it.

Frederick Fraser, stretched out on a low couch against a wooden bulkhead of the houseboat's long and narrow stateroom, glanced at the red and green umbrella. 'What d'you think this is, mate? The nineteenth hole?'

'That's the Spanish Open, isn't it?' asked Forbes, ignoring the remark and stripping off his raincoat. 'I just came from Spain. Beautiful weather.' Sitting down, he removed his left shoe and his wet sock, then went back to the corner under the companionway and wrung the sock out into the little puddle left by his umbrella.

'Make yourself at home, do.'

'Is there some way we can dry this out?' asked Forbes, holding up the sock.

'That might be arranged.' Fraser held out a beefy, gnarled hand. 'What's all this, then? I ain't seen hide nor hair of you for months, then you barge in here using the place like a bleedin' Chinese laundry.'

'It *is* a barge, isn't it?'

'Very funny,' Fraser grunted as he got to his bare feet, wrapped the dragon more firmly around him, took the sock and disappeared with it through a door. He returned half a minute later. 'I put it on a pot of coffee. Should do the trick when it starts boilin'.' His smallish, bright, shrewd eyes bored into those of Forbes, who was grinning at him. 'Where, when, and how much?'

'Did I say anything about . . . ?'

'You didn't come 'ere in a tempest to admire me roses, did you, mate?'

'No.'

'How's that gorgeous bit of crumpet of yours, by the way?'

'Christ, Freddie, she's my wife.'

He chuckled. 'Married means you don't get it up as much as you used to, don't it?'

Forbes shook his head. 'Jesus,' he sighed. But he wanted this irreverent cockney on his team, needed him badly. Fraser, shot through the shoulder, competent and tough enough to doctor himself, had been one of the survivors at Matagalpa. He was utterly reliable, brave to the point of insanity, one of the finest shots with side-arms Forbes knew of; give him a Smith & Wesson 459, he could pick a wart off your nose at two hundred paces. A shelf running almost the length of the stateroom was crammed with his shooting trophies.

'Just kiddin'. You always was a stud. You're probably givin' it one every night.'

'Do me a favour, Freddie. Can it.'

'Fair enough. So, what's up?'

'The Costa del Sol. Pronto – which means two or three days depending when I've got all my team together. Twenty K.'

Fraser's jaw dropped open. 'Workin' for the Bill, are you? Ronnie Knight chucked in the towel last year . . .'

'For the Kuwaiti government,' Forbes broke in.

'Saddam don't take holidays, he's been advised to stay at home.'

There was a loud whistling sound from beyond the door. Fraser took his solid, forty-year-old frame through to the head, which divided the stateroom from where he slept, in the stubby-nosed prow where the bed was never made and the sheets seldom changed. As he went he said: 'We may as well have some coffee while your sock's dryin'.'

He was back within a minute, bringing two small cups of thick, black, percolated coffee. He gave one to Forbes. 'The way you like it. I remember: three sugars.'

'You planning on being my batman?'

'You need one. Your fuckin' sock's stinkin' out my kitchen.'

'Balls. I wear a clean pair every day.'

'What's the SP then?'

'There's a Saudi living down near Marbella. A sheikh. We have to parcel him up and deliver him to Kuwait. Breathing.'

'Sounds good.'

'You're with me?'

Fraser poured a few drops of Lepanto brandy, from Jerez, close to the Costa del Sol, into his coffee and offered the bottle to Forbes. 'They don't drink, do they, the Saudis? Against their religion.'

'That's right.' Forbes swallowed some coffee, then filled the cup to the brim with Lepanto.

'I never did care much for a man who doesn't drink. Count me in, Steve.'

*   *   *

There was one more man on Forbes's list on that English summer's day designed to send anyone with the time and money scuttling with their bedraggled tail between their legs to where Forbes and his crew were about to travel. He was the last of the six who lived in London, Tristram MacDowell, a rangy Scot from Edinburgh with a semi-detached house and a semi-detached wife in Muswell Hill; an expert in all aspects of unarmed combat; a man as hard as a marble statue who could kill with two well-placed fingers; a grower of prize hyacinths and carnations.

As Forbes's taxi splashed its way northwards from Little Venice. Leila, her mission to recruit a far-flung, hoped-for member of the team of abductors, was being welcomed into a cottage in a cobbled street in Ross-on-Wye.

Johnnie Johnson was thirty-seven, six-two, broad-shouldered and blessed with a Clark Gable grin which was at least fifty per cent of the secret of his remarkable success with the fair sex. He was a complicated fusion of characters. There was Johnnie the novelist, with three, disappointingly selling thrillers to his credit. Johnnie the equestrian was a rider of consummate skill, many times winner of cross-country events and gymkhanas, and occasional movie stunt horseman. There was Johnnie the professional guitarist; Johnnie the proprietor of a small, not vastly profitable drinking club. And there was Johnnie the cool contract killer with an SAS background. He was also the only one of two people who had been with Forbes and Leila during the aborted Saudi gold robbery who had lived to tell the tale.

Johnnie greeted Leila with his infamous grin and a bear-hug which had little to do with comradely love. He kissed her on either cheek, his lips lingering longer than was customary on the Continent.

'Down, boy,' she grunted, struggling to free herself.

He let go of her cuddly little body with reluctance, holding her at arm's length and studying her with rapacious eye; she even managed to look ravishing in a dripping-wet raincoat and with a scarf over her head.

'Stephen must have lost his marbles, sending you to me,' he said. He held out a slim, well-manicured hand. 'The coat.'

She stripped it off and gave it to him and he hung it over a curly-topped wooden stand. She untied her headscarf. Her shiny tresses fell loose, tumbling over black leather and white, silk-covered shoulders. With the leather waistcoat and frilly blouse, she was wearing skin-tight, black leather trousers and high-heeled, patent boots selected because rain rolled off them.

'Stephen's marbles are perfectly in order,' she told him. 'What's more, you're supposed to be a buddy of his, so lay off.'

'Sure, but,' he groaned as he ran his long-lashed, baby-brown eyes up and down her body, 'have you any idea what you *look* like? Bloody hell. They don't build them like you here in Ross-on-Wye.'

'Remember Emma Peel?' – *The Avengers* had recently been rerun on TV – 'this is the sort of combat gear she wears. You just watch it, buster.'

He laughed. 'Come on in and sit down.'

In point of fact she was already in, for the cottage had no hallway, the front door opening straight on to a charming living-room with a low, wonky, black-beamed ceiling. The room's dominant feature was a large inglenook adorned with gleaming horse brasses and two hunting horns. Johnnie's predatory eyes rarely left Leila as he poured them some ice-cold Chablis.

'I would never have imagined you living here,' she said as he handed her a glass and sat next to her on the flower-patterned sofa. She was remembering how he had single-mindedly, cleverly, planned and organized the blowing up of an entire building in Wigmore Street more than two years earlier in order to bury the Saudi gold-filled safe which they planned to cut into from below. 'I mean, it's great, this part of the world is beautiful, but I see you in a penthouse pad off Soho Square somewhere with Andy Warhols on the walls – not a chintzy cottage.'

'So do I – one part of me, that is. But the horsey part dominates and it can't be satisfied in a city.'

The way he was staring at her as he took a long swig of wine, he looked as if he was going to pounce. She shifted her backside into the corner of the sofa, recalling how she had been obliged to fend him off once before. He kept his hands to himself, but his eyes were invading her, making her nervous; the problem was she found the man extremely attractive, which conflicted with her loyalty to Stephen; physical loyalty that was, but there was not much she could do about the mental variety.

You bastard, she thought. Boy, could I . . . she hastily shut the idea out of her mind. 'Message received loud and clear, Johnnie,' she said. 'Now, do me a favour, uh? Behave yourself. I'm a cross-eyed, one-legged hunchback, right? With leprosy. Let's talk business.'

Johnnie sighed the sigh of a fat man on a strict diet contemplating a chocolate gâteau. 'There should be a law against chicks like you. Shoot.'

*   *   *

Tristram MacDowell had at last signed on after making a demand for more money which had been refused. The other two were in different parts of England, both of which could be reached comfortably in one day's driving.

There was a near-miraculous metamorphosis in the weather the following day. The clouds went into retreat, the sun streamed down, the pavements dried and Londoners smiled once again – it was amazing what sunshine did for people's mood.

'To hell with it,' said Forbes, as he and Leila dressed for breakfast, 'I'm going to hire a Merc for the day.' They were in the most expensive hotel Hammid Mullah would allow – no Savoy suite this time, but a room in the Great Cumberland on the Bayswater Road.

Leila tutted. 'Mr Mullah's going to have kittens.'

'Let him. If I have to, I'll pay for it myself.'

They went together, up the M1 to Birmingham, where he hired the lugubrious Albert Tidy, the only other member of his squad in Nicaragua to have survived the carnage in 1987. There was nothing astonishingly out of the ordinary about Albert: he was wiry, tough, dependable manpower, a Brummie who, despite his doleful looks, made you feel comfortable to know you had him on your team.

They had lunch in a country pub, Forbes downing most of a bottle of Beaujolais and then a schooner of Courvoisier with coffee afterwards. When, without rancour, Leila warned him about being over the limit, he told her perfectly soberly what she knew he would: he didn't give a toss about breathalizers, and he would tell the bastards exactly where to stuff them.

They drove on up to Chester to seek out the final man on the list, Luis Roldán, a Colombian who, curiously, bore the same name as the fugitive, disgraced ex-chief of the Madrid Guardia Civil.

Just short of Chester, Forbes pulled the white Mercedes 380SL on to the hard shoulder to consult his map. Then he drove on for two and a half miles to take a turn-off. They went through a small, tidy village where he again stopped to look at the map, then out of it and into an oak and beech-lined forest lane.

'Tell me about this guy,' said Leila as they turned left at a crossroads with a white signpost. 'Didn't you say you've never met him?'

'Yeah. Curious history. He's young, about thirty. He was a rising star in the band of one of the Colombian drug barons until a couple of years back. The boss raped his sister and he got his own back by volunteering information to the CIA. Then he was recruited by Charlie Powers as

92

one of the squad of mercenaries employed by the Yanks to bust the big boss's factory. Charlie told me about him last time we were in London.'

Forbes slowed the Merc to a crawl, then nosed it down a narrow track with the sign 'Bramble Caravan Site' at its beginning.

'And he lives *here*?' asked Leila.

'He's an illegal alien. The raid was successful in that they burned the factory down, but the baron and crew escaped. Luis got out of Colombia fast and he daren't go back. They'd find out soon enough and they'd kill him – slowly, I imagine.'

They arrived at the site. It was orderly, with well-kept caravans with neat little gardens around them, many of the caravans resting on small brick walls.

Leila wanted to know why Forbes wanted Roldán.

'We're going to need someone who speaks Spanish. And Charlie assured me that he's a truly unusual breed of fighting animal.' He parked and they left the car to walk to an information office, a prefabricated affair painted an unlovely shade of pink.

A taciturn, rat-faced woman – with ratty hair to match – formidable custodian of the information, sale and rental office, pointed out the caravan which Roldán had rented months before under the name of Luis Rodríguez. It was surrounded by pots of geraniums. It was locked and he was not at home.

'I'm not his keeper, am I?' Rat-face told them. Then, grudgingly, she added: 'He's probably down at the river, fishing.'

The river was at the end of a half-mile-long woodland lane which for the final hundred yards became a well-trodden track across a sparsely grassed field. There was just one man by the water. He had black, shiny, slicked-back hair and he was sitting, rod in hand, with his back to them.

They stole very quietly up to him.

'Luis Roldán?' asked Forbes, when they were almost upon him.

The man's reaction was instantaneous. He was on his feet and haring for his life along the river bank, fishing gear abandoned, before Forbes and Leila had taken another step. 'Cool it, Luis,' Forbes bellowed after him. 'Charlie Powers sent me.' The man stopped, turned around slowly and looked at them with dark, suspicious eyes from a hundred yards away; he had covered that distance in fifteen seconds. 'You no *policía*?' he called out.

With his heavy build, concrete face and pale-blue shirt, Forbes could have been; plain-clothes policemen and villains often remarkably resembled one another – not to say that Stephen Forbes was exactly a villain, but neither could he be described as of unblemished character. Leila on the other hand, in her pale-mauve blouse, breasts temptingly thrusting, her white miniskirt and snowy Reebok trainers with rolled-down socks to match the blouse, was nobody but a fool's idea of a lady in blue.

'Shit, no,' said Forbes. 'Charlie told me all about you. I can probably use you.' He picked up the man's rod. A bright red float, at full line's stretch down-river in the clear, sluggish water, was bobbing violently. He held the rod towards Roldán as he walked cautiously back towards them. 'You've got a fish by the looks of it.'

'Who are you?' asked the Colombian, reaching them. Taking the rod, he began reeling the fish in.

Forbes told him.

Roldán appraised Leila with that familiar, masculine look to which she was so accustomed. Latins were usually slightly more obvious, and so was this one, but at least he made it quick. His eyes wandered back to the float as the hook left the water with a fish only a little larger than a minnow wriggling on it. 'Charlie Powers, he good chap,' he said, his accent thick. He carefully separated the fish from the hook and threw it back in the river.

'The best. I've worked with him.'

'What you want?' he said as he sat on the bank and began rebaiting the hook.

Forbes and Leila squatted on either side of him, and Forbes outlined his proposition, omitting the target's name and exact location. In Spain, he said, they needed someone who spoke Spanish.

'Charlie told me you're brilliant with small arms,' Forbes mentioned, his brief outline finished.

'Small arms? What is small arms?'

'Any small weapon.'

'Ah, *sí*. Here.' Roldán thrust the cork-covered handle of his rod into Forbes's hand. Then he dug him slyly in his ribs with his elbow – a Spanish habit which, along with people touching you as they spoke, Forbes loathed, though this time he ignored it. 'Watch. Watch the water.'

Forbes and Leila stared at the river without having any idea what to expect. What happened next was so fast that it was over almost before they were aware of it. There was a blur of movement as Roldán snatched a knife from a sheath at his belt and flung it at the water. It flashed a split second's sunlight, cut cleanly into the river, vanished and reappeared seconds later, its lightly varnished, wooden handle bobbing on the surface like a float and drifting downstream. The Colombian angled a long-handled net under it and fished it out.

An eight-inch, red-finned roach was impaled, dead, on the shiny blade of the throwing knife.

It took a lot to impress Forbes, but he muttered: 'Jesus Christ,' as Leila whistled her amazement.

Roldán grinned flatly, showing perfectly white and even teeth. 'You lucky you not policeman. I get you through the heart at fifty paces.'

'I'm impressed,' said Forbes. 'Charlie was right about you. So why do you bother with a rod?'

'I like to fish, no? Fishing is slow. Fishing you think a lot.' He pulled the roach off the knife and dropped it into a plastic container. His gaze was attracted to movement a short way along the river-bank, upstream. He irritated Forbes with another dig in the ribs. 'You both keeping very still. Me, I show you other thing.'

The Colombian's swarthy hand closed over a tennis-ball-sized pebble. Slowly, he drew back his arm.

The grey-furred rabbit was maybe thirty metres distant, hopping slowly away from the river. Roldán hurled the stone with deadly accuracy. It smacked into the side of the animal's head and it dropped in its tracks, twitched three times and died.

'You don't really have a great need for money, do you, son?' observed Forbes. 'You can feed yourself just sitting here.'

'I am needing twenty grands.'

'You've got them, Luis, you've got them. Consider them in the bank.'

Later, after a splendid meal in an olde-worlde restaurant accompanied by, for Forbes, just the right amount to drink, while speeding south, turning over his plans in his mind and considering the merits of a team which he thought exceptional, he found himself becoming more and more aware of Leila's shapely, miniskirted legs and less and less of the motorway ahead. His driving went on to automatic pilot as the inner excitement at what he had achieved so far and at the tricky task ahead of him performed the tantalizing trick of sparking his libido.

'Uh, where are you taking us, Stephen?' asked Leila, as he took an exit road. 'London was straight ahead. You couldn't miss it.'

'London can wait,' he murmured. The growl in his voice turned her head sharply to him. That, and the glint in his eye, told her exactly what was on the menu; her inner thighs twitched. She laid a hand, high up, on one of his.

'Horny sod,' she muttered happily.

Horny indeed. Two minutes along the busy road he pulled the Merc off into a hedged country lane and drove slowly until he found a recess in front of the closed gate of a field. He parked, then switched off the lights and the engine.

'Back-seat job,' he said, his belly tense with need as he opened the door. 'If I've got to pay through the nose for this heap, let's make the most of it.'

9

There was perhaps little need for the extremes of caution to which Forbes went in bringing his team into Spain. But he was a perfectionist and he had seen and heard of deals being ruined because of the tiniest slip-up. The mercenary history of one or other of his six men – or all of them for that matter – could be on airport computer records. He had no objection to them travelling with their real names on the tickets and with genuine passports but for all six of them, together with himself and Leila, to pop off down to Málaga together – a cosy little convention of soldiers of fortune – could be courting disaster before the mission had hardly even begun.

Nobody travelled together except Mr and Mrs Forbes. Only one person went on one flight and only two of them, with the exception of the happy couple, flew into Málaga. The others went respectively to Seville and Gibraltar. They were each billeted in different smallish but comfortable hotels and Forbes and Leila again checked into a Marbella Club bungalow, this one just as attractive as the other had been, with a pool and a jacaranda tree and the intriguing name of Casa Puck.

The initial briefing took place late on the morning after their arrival, at the bungalow. They arrived at Casa Puck at prearranged five-minute intervals, each in his own hire car and each neatly dressed per Forbes's instructions; should any of them get stopped by a security guard during their short walk from the car park down the flower-lined lane to the bungalow, he wanted their appearance to be perfectly respectable.

None of them was questioned. Had they been, they were visiting Forbes and that checked out OK. By eleven-thirty they were sitting around on wicker chairs on the terrace of Casa Puck, and Hammid Mullah was solemnly handing out fat manila envelopes, each stuffed with £5000. Only MacDowell bothered to count the money.

'It's all there,' he announced as Mullah was about to leave.

'Are you quite sure, Mr MacDowell?' asked the Kuwaiti coldly, his accountant's nature offended. 'Perhaps you'd like to count it again?'

'Funny sort of a bird,' commented the Scot when, making a business of leaving, Mullah marched smartly in through the open terrace doors, across the lounge, and banged the front door behind him.

'Annoying little bugger,' said Forbes. 'But at least he coughts up on the dot.'

Luis Roldán was the only one of the others to have opened his envelope. He was thumbing through the notes, smiling broadly. 'Five grands,' he mumbled. 'Is good.'

'Now all you've got to do is earn it,' Forbes told him. 'When you get the other fifteen you can stop massacring bunnies for supper.'

'We're not expected to cover our hotel exes with this, are we?' asked Freddie.

'The accountant will take care of all that shit.'

'We sound like a bleedin' corporation.'

'And we have to run at least as smooth as one, if not smoother. And you will – you're going to make a cup-winning team.' He looked at them briefly, one by one. 'OK, you've got your readies, now to business.' Picking up a pack of photographs from where they had been lying face down on a glass-topped coffee table, he distributed two, each pair the same, to all of them. One was a close-up of Sulman's face, taken through the sheikh's car window by Forbes with a telephoto lens from the depths of the wood. The other, shot from the same position, was of the usual three-car convoy emerging through the elephant gates. Only the little red Merc was entirely in view – the bodyguards' cars were each partially obscured by intervening trees – but the prints were large and perfectly in focus.

'Bulletproof glass,' remarked Guy Keegan.

Forbes glanced sharply at him. 'How can you tell?'

'I couldn't tell you about the Cadi, because the windows are black. But the other two, to be sure. It has that certain glint to it.'

'Nothing that a point-50-calibre shell couldn't pierce,' commented Johnnie, the first words from his mouth since being introduced to the others, none of whom he had met before. His eyes had been on Leila on and off – more on than off – ever since his arrival. Dressed in tight little black shorts, gold, flat shoes and a white halter top, she looked good enough to eat – any way that took your fancy. Johnnie was saddled with a case of the galloping hots for her which he was afraid he was going to find difficult to control.

'So would a lot of other heavy ammunition,' said Forbes. 'But we'll be trying to avoid a slaughter if we can. This is a kidnapping, not a *coup d'état*.' He distributed more photographs, these aerial shots of Casa al-Riyadh. 'Security cameras with ears cover every inch of ground around the house – and the beach. It's lit up at night, there are emergency searchlights and

a siren, and there's double fencing at the front
and a dog run with some affectionate Rottweilers
around the rest of it. I don't know the total of
heavies, but I'd say at the very minimum fifteen. It
isn't exactly your Aunty Mabel's country cottage
with roses round the door.'

'And what was that blarney about a doddle you
came out with when you conned me into coming
down here?' asked Guy Keegan.

Forbes stared at him, his expression unread-
able. 'I think,' he said slowly after a long pause,
'but I haven't made up my mind, that we're
going to have to snatch him from his Merc.
Fortunately he's a sociable little sod. He goes
out a great deal.'

'Not exactly unaccompanied,' pointed out
Albert Tidy. His face was set in its usual mask
of doom. 'Four men in the Merc. Do you have any
idea how many there would be in the Cadi?'

'Six,' said Forbes. 'I've tailed him twice during
the day. Each time, the heavies were left on the
drives of friends' houses while he had lunch. Six
men in the Cadillac, playing cards, wandering
around, lethargic minders without much expec-
tation that anything was going to happen. It's
fairly safe to assume that Sulman's a man of
strict habits as far as his security is concerned.
I imagine he's always got ten men with him.'

'Quite a bloody show,' said Albert. 'More

like a fucking president than an arms dealer.'

'Curious little irony if some of the weapons we've held in our lily-white hands in the past had been supplied by him,' said Johnnie. His eyes roved over Leila's pressed-together knees, traversed her breasts, lingered on her face, then flickered to Forbes.

He was far from blind, but Forbes nourished the conceit that nobody but him stood the ghost of a chance with Leila; make love to them as often and as interestingly as possible had been his lifelong motto, and they won't stray – not unless they're of the nymphomaniac persuasion. There was a lot of truth in that and that's how it was with Leila. Let Gable-grin Johnnie have his eyeful and lust as much as he liked. Tough shit.

'So, what's the next step, boyo?' asked Keegan.

Forbes looked long and hard at him. 'We're old pals, you and me, Guy,' he told him. 'Nevertheless, from now on I'm your commander, not your boyo. OK? You know why.'

Keegan took the admonition unflinchingly: Forbes was right, there had to be discipline and respect within the group. This was no kids' game. Far from it – it looked as if it was going to be a keg of dynamite. 'OK, boss,' he said. 'Point taken.'

'Good. And that goes for the rest of you. Stick to calling me Steve, or Stephen, but think

General. The next step is more reconnaissance, Guy. You're the electronics department. Take a close look at the shots of the house. Can you organize a tap on the phones?'

'With all those security cameras it's going to be a problem. I'll have to get my arse down there, so I will. Take a closer look.'

'Do it after lunch.'

'Fair enough, General.'

Forbes sighed. 'And don't take the piss.'

10

It was the Feria de San Bernabé in Marbella, a fair lasting a whole week. While not a man with a great love of mixing with the *hoi polloi*, Sheikh Sulman was a passionate aficionado of falconry, like so many Saudis, and that afternoon there was a show involving Andalusian horses and falcons. It was being held as part of the fair celebrations in a field in a largely forested area behind Marbella known as Los Nagueles.

The sheikh attended, cocooned by his usual retinue of bodyguards. They were among the crowd at one of the rickety wooden barrier rails of the temporary arena set up for the show when it began. The arena was roughly the same size as that of the average gymkhana. The grass had been cropped short and spread with a thick layer of sand which was already trodden in after an opening exhibition of dressage performed by some of the world-famous leaping horses of Jerez, and soiled here and there with dung.

Sulman and his bodyguards appeared as out

of place among the summery, boisterous, mostly Spanish crowd as would have a group of grey-suited Japanese businessmen on the beach of a tropical island. He had a change of female companion with him. She was not quite as plump as the previous one, but she was curvaceous enough in all the right places – especially the coveted derrière – to suit his taste. She was very young, a blonde with hair which fell straight to her waist, and pale-blue eyes whose frequent laughter failed to disguise a brittleness brought to them by her lifestyle. Her name was Marian, and she had been seduced from her Amsterdam hooker's shop window by the sheikh's full-time pimp with the promise of more money than she could hope to earn in a year.

Apart from the girl, Sulman was surrounded by large and threatening-looking men who dwarfed him, the usual number of ten, whom he changed around from time to time to keep them on their toes. He was aware that to be accompanied by so many heavies wherever he went was a monumental exaggeration – especially here in Spain where, deadly enemies or no, he was highly unlikely to be subjected to an all-out attack. But it gave him a warm feeling inside, a feeling, moreover, of power. He disliked being small and enjoyed bossing huge men around. Much more, distantly related to the Saudi royals, he carried a king-sized chip on his bird-sized shoulder that he was not one of them. Having more bodyguards than any of them except benevolent King Fahd – who did not particularly want them but had them thrust upon him out of necessity – did much to boost his deflated ego.

There had been a lull in the proceedings in the arena, and the air was full of the typical noise generated by a Spanish fiesta crowd. Good-natured squabbling – though a non-Spaniard could be forgiven for believing they were about to tear one another's throats out – loud laughter, shouting, the screaming of the loved-to-death kids – all this racket was rivalled by a pair of loudspeakers whose tweeters and woofers had seen better days blaring flamenco and Sevillian music which was blurry and cracked all around the edges. Suddenly there was an expectant hush following a just understandable loudspeaker announcement echoing and booming off La Concha mountain, which reared rockily up to the immediate north.

A single rider on a magnificent, white Andalusian stallion – a noble breed with Arab blood in its veins – cantered into the ring and brought his mount to a slithering stop in its centre, his right arm held high. The rider was dressed in gleaming black leather boots, cream leather chaps, a frilly, black silk shirt, a grey bolero jacket and a flat grey hat with a black band in which there was a red carnation. His raised arm was clad to the elbow in a worn, grey leather glove, and perching on his half-fisted hand, hooded, attached to the glove with a thin silver chain, was a stately, metre-high falcon.

To thunderous applause from the audience the rider reared his stallion on to its hind legs and turned it through three hundred and sixty degrees as he proudly exhibited the majestic bird of prey, which sat still and upright on his glove. Sulman's normally impassive, dark-chocolate-coloured eyes glinted with excitement; this was a sport which was part of his soul, something his father had initiated him into in the desert near Riyadh when he was three, long before the real significance of King Ibn Saud's having sold the first oil concessions to America ten years earlier in 1935 was truly understood. He kept several falcons in his palatial house in Saudi Arabia, though he was seldom there. They were reared and trained to perfection, for he had spent at least a million dollars on them over the years.

As the stallion was stilled, another rider galloped into the ring. He reined in his horse close to the first and began swinging a small black pouch on a lace around his head. The leather bag contained raw meat, and the man was impregnating the air with its scent. The bird, which had been kept hungry, tensed; his long, yellowy talons bit into the glove.

This was the moment when Forbes, unaware of the presence of Sulman and crew, found a place for himself and Leila at the rails diagonally across from the sheikh. Also a lover of falconry, he had watched it many times in Saudi, in Dubai and in the United Arab Emirates. As he leant on the wobbly rail, the second rider ceased swinging the pouch and unclipped a cage attached to his saddle. Inside was a forlorn and solitary sparrow.

The falconer removed the hood from his charge's beady eyes, and the bird stretched its huge, fawny-feathered wings, while its feathers puffed on its neck. But it did not attempt to fly. It knew it would not get far until the chain was released.

The supreme drama, as dramatic as the clean kill of a brave fighting bull, was about to unfold. The falconer unclipped the chain and threw his arm high. The bird soared a hundred metres into the air, hovered for a moment, then began to circle. The other man uncaged the sparrow, which shot off towards the mountain.

With an extraordinary yet apparently effortless turn of speed, the falcon swooped, a tawny blur. The sparrow sensed it coming. It swerved to one side, then the other, but it had as much chance of escape as a cow lumbering across the path of an express train. Squawking terror in the vicious grip of the talons, it was brought to earth in the arena, where the falcon's hooked, razor-sharp beak ripped it to pieces.

'Wow,' said Leila. She shivered.

Across from her, Sheikh Sulman's eyes were afire. The kill invariably brought him a rush of excitement. As with Forbes, but in more perverted a fashion, that rush went to his loins. His brown, spidery hand slipped from where it had been resting on Marian's waist to her well-rounded, tightly cotton-clad buttocks. His gaze slithered from the greedily feeding falcon to her backside, where it dwelt; when the show was over he was going to take her home, strip her bare and have that bottom. And how he was going to have it.

'Fuck me,' muttered Forbes.

'*Please*, lover,' said Leila, mock-crossly, 'how many more times have I to beg you to . . . ?'

'He's here. The son of a bitch is right here.'

'What?' Her eyes followed his. There he was, with his thugs and his girlfriend, on the southern side of the arena, the distant coastline and the sparkling Mediterranean his impressive backdrop. 'Oh.'

'Had I known.'

'Well, you do now. Go and show him your ID and ask him to kindly step this way, sir.'

The falcon had been lured back on to his handler's glove with the offer of raw red meat – somewhat more appetizing than the paltry, stringy flesh of the sparrow. The chain had been clipped back in place, and to sustained applause the rider was cantering off, the bird unhooded and chewing hungrily away as a second falconer with a bird just slightly smaller than the first elegantly danced his chestnut mare to the centre of the arena.

Forbes tensed. His gaze had caught the glint of sunlight on something white in the vicinity of Sulman. He looked harder. Two bandages thoroughly encased the thumb and bottom half and wrist of each of a pair of meaty hands which were resting on the middle arena rail close to the sheikh. Forbes studied the leathery face of the man to whom the hands belonged; the man who had destroyed his film and who had been one of those who had killed the poor bastard drunk. The heavy whom he had KO'd in Da Paulo's bar before breaking his thumbs.

One does not easily forget a face which was the last thing seen in close-up in a mirror before being slugged. It tends to engrave itself on one's memory. As Forbes was deciding it might be a wise move to remove that face from the Arab's field of vision, it was spotted. The man looked him directly in the eye. He glanced briefly at Leila, whose elbow was propped on Forbes's shoulder. He looked back at Forbes searchingly. His small, unattractive eyes got smaller. Moving away from the barrier, he spoke urgently to a colleague, whose eyes jerked towards Forbes and Leila. The two men began to hurriedly push their way through the crush.

'Er ... red alert,' grunted Forbes. 'We've gone.'

He grabbed Leila's hand and hustled her off through the crowds, away from the car park, which was wide and open and where they would be spotted. They would almost certainly get away, but the number of their hired Twingo – a hideous shade of green this time – would be noted. And it was in Leila's name with the Marbella Club's address displayed.

They slipped unseen into the dense pine forest. They would work their way around to the car park from its other side, through the trees, and leave when the heat was off. But to have been recognized by the bodyguard was hardly the best of news.

The heavies gave up after some twenty minutes of searching; it was evident that their quarry had melted away. Back at the rails, the bandaged thug informed the sheikh that the man responsible for his nasty injury had been in the vicinity.

'But you still don't know *why* he did it, do you, Zakhr?' Sulman asked him coldly, in Arabic. He cared little; hoods were hoods, they were as thick as planks, always getting into bother.

'I do now,' said Zakhr. 'I think I do.'

'How's that?'

'A couple of weeks or so back? Outside the house? A man with a camera. With a girl. I screwed up his film.'

'And?'

'I didn't recognize him when he slugged me. He didn't look like the same geezer. But I just recognized the bird. She was with him that day. He was dressed kind of weird the first time. They went all around the house.'

Sulman frowned. 'I see. And he broke your thumbs because you ruined his film. You're positive it was the same man? And the girl?'

'It was him, yeah. And the chick without doubt. I was watching her through the telescope. Hot stuff. Great piece of arse.'

Sheikh Sulman quickly turned the unwelcome information over in his nimble brain. Then he had been right: that odd little series of events two weeks or so before had been significant. He was being watched. And the watcher was tough enough to put one of his heavies out of action and dislocate his thumbs.

He had already tightened up his security; now he would have to tighten it even more. And he would use that other clever little ploy of his, recently invented, more often.

'Good work, Zakhr,' he said. His eyes flickered to Marian. His perverted need was even stronger. His hand clawed into her buttock. 'We're leaving,' he muttered.

11

By far the most efficient way to bug a telephone was to get co-operation from the local exchange to put the line out of action, then go into the house disguised as a repairman and contrive an SF that could be activated over short distances using short-wave, high-frequency megacycles, into the receiver. That way a room would be permanently covered and all conversation – not just on the telephone – occurring in it could be recorded.

Keegan was musing on the impracticability of this as, in swimming shorts and rubber flip-flops, and with a towel draped over one shoulder and cased binoculars over the other, he took a tour around Casa al-Riyadh similar to that of Forbes and Leila on their first day. Foolishly, he had not brought a shirt with him. The late June sunshine was deceptive. By the time he had ambled past the naked sun worshippers, trying like a good Catholic to avoid the sin of prurience and failing badly, his pale and freckly, typical Irish skin was beginning to burn.

There were two major stumbling blocks to the installation of an SF, the necessary gear for which he could have parcelled and flown out to him from London via jet service. The co-operation of the San Pedro exchange could only be obtained by someone successfully passing himself off as a police or government agent, and since the only member of their team who spoke Spanish did so with a heavy Colombian accent this ruse seemed doomed to failure. Secondly, even if this succeeded there was the probability that any engineer tinkering with the telephones of so heavily guarded a man as Sheikh Sulman would have his every move carefully watched.

Keegan would have to get a tap directly from a telephone wire. If it was underground, that was no easy task. On the other hand, if, as in the case of many houses in the area, there was a visible line hooking into the main system before it went underground, there was the problem of the security cameras.

As he walked past the villa's beach frontage he set off the Rottweilers. He had had a fear of dogs ever since as a kid one of those black-and-white, ubiquitous Emerald Isle mongrels with strains of setter in them had playfully ripped his left earlobe half off. He hurried down the beach and ankle deep into the sea, splashing eastwards until the Rottweilers decided his unwelcome, alien-scented presence was far enough past the house for them to quieten down again.

Occasionally peeping at the villa through his binoculars, looking for wires, Keegan wandered up towards the highway on the far side of the abandoned urbanization site from it. Then, as he took the road which closed in on Casa al-Riyadh to pass by the gates, Sulman's motorcade, rushing the sheikh and his highly paid whore home for him to have his sodomitic way with her, whispered out of the wood towards him.

Keegan reacted brilliantly. From the far corner of the hedge, letting his shoulders droop, he stood and goggled at the cars like a yokel, his jaw slack, eyes wide, as the electronic elephants opened and swallowed them up.

Just another dumb tourist. Sulman's goons paid scant attention to the Irishman. But the sheikh himself, despite his panting libido, wondered about him. He was on his guard, wary about anybody and everybody crossing his path, even such an obvious holidaymaker. As he drove through the second gate he spat the command into his walkie-talkie to have Keegan's every move monitored.

Keegan located the telephone wire. Attached to a high pole near the gates, it was strung with barely any slack from pole to pole, cutting out at an angle towards the highway and skirting the wood. He followed it for a short distance until he was almost in the trees, where he stopped and used his binoculars.

In the turret, the telescope was trained on him.

'Just some nutty bird-watcher,' said the Arab whose eye was at the viewing end.

A few minutes later, near the eastern edge of the wood, from where he could see the telephone wire, Keegan began studying the trees. An idea was beginning to take shape in his mind. A perhaps dangerous idea, and the whole business was going to be decidedly uncomfortable, but it did offer a solution of sorts to his problem. Better perhaps if the wire had been underground, but then there would have been the difficulty of electronic detection.

The equipment he was going to need was specialized, though not particularly rare. Since his Spanish was non-existent, he would take Luis Roldán on a shopping trip for the necessary items.

'I'm not so sure we should be this friendly with him,' grumbled Lord Sandhurst as he drove his lady wife through the little wood just before dusk. 'I mean, one has one's reputation to consider.'

'Don't be such a bloody ass, Charles,' she replied. 'I like him. I really do. There's something almost hypnotic about him. We shall refer to him as Y in the future. Y for Yasser. It rather suits him.'

'How about TT for dry?' Lord Sandhurst performed the trick of unscrewing its silver cap with the fingers of the hand he was holding it in and took a quick swig from the leather-bound hip-flask of Stolichnaya which he was about to smuggle into the booze-free house: the sheikh, his illicit dealing in arms and his sexual proclivities notwithstanding, remained a strict Muslim. Sandhurst brought his beloved, burgundy-coloured vintage Bentley to a stop in front of the elephant gates and tooted its horn – a wholly unnecessary action since the Bentley had been on TV since emerging from the wood. The well-oiled gates swung open silently.

Two hundred and fifty metres to the west, black-clad and sharing an indentation in a scrubby field with a dozing donkey, flat on his belly, Forbes observed the arrival of Lord and Lady Sandhurst with keen interest. Having already tracked them down – but not actually met them – as the owners of the house he had watched Sulman visit from the Comanche aircraft, he had made it his business to find out a little about them; they were pillars of English society on the coast, much photographed and gossiped about – the very epitome of upper-class respectability.

Strange bedfellows for the gun-running sheikh, thought Forbes as the elephants trundled back together.

The Bentley lumbered through the second set of gates and on past the Olympic-sized, floodlit pool, to the house. Extraordinarily, there was a man in a peaked cap and white gloves to open Lady Sandhurst's door; there was a bulge under his black cotton jacket which she failed to notice.

The front doors of the house had a cladding of beaten copper studded with brass. The well-travelled Sandhursts had never in their experience come across another home with a Venetian cut-crystal chandelier hanging outside it. A furnishing supremely elegant when properly placed, here it looked tawdry and vulgar. It was switched on, though there remained a smidgen of light from the vanished sun, and its hundreds of pear-sized pendants were shaking and tinkling in the evening breeze, throwing shimmering spots over the uneven copper doors in front of which it hung. It irritated the Sandhursts, yet failed to surprise them; this was their second visit to Casa al-Riyadh and the chandelier was merely typical of the rampant bad taste — at least by Western standards — throughout the villa.

Within the sprawling, hotel-sized foyer, with its central fish-pond full of some of the fattest goldfish the Sandhursts had ever set eyes upon and an illuminated fountain which softly played Arab music while constantly changing colour, was the usual reception committee. Six burly men with the bulge of shoulder-holstered pistols beneath their neat, white shirts were arranged in a semicircle around the curved, mauve-velvet-lined rear wall of the entrance hall. They stood erect, their huge shoulders back, legs spread and with their hands behind their backs like junior ratings welcoming an admiral or other distinguished visitor aboard ship. Their gazes were fixed somewhere above the visitors' heads as the Sandhursts were ushered between them and through a pair of gold-leaf-veneered doors by a seemingly perfect English butler wearing a black tailcoat and an expression snooty enough to be worthy of Jeeves himself.

Sulman was dressed by some of the world's greatest clothiers, yet, as always, had managed to pick sadly conflicting combinations. This evening it was a chalk-striped suit with a horizontally striped pale-pink shirt, a bright flowered tie, brown and white brogues and his inevitable little silk, flat hat, this one green with a pearl sitting dead centre on its top. He greeted them in a drawing-room which was an interior decorator's nightmare – marble statues vied for attention with ultra-modern, plexiglass and chrome sculptures; delicate, period furniture sat side by side with contemporary trash; Chinese, Persian and Spanish rugs in clashing colours littered the three hundred square metres of white-marble floor; and the lighting was at once from chandeliers, chrome spotlights and converted oil lamps. Until one got used to it, it was dizzying.

Lord Sandhurst had remarked to his wife after their previous visit to this Alice-in-Wonderland villa that the bloody man must be 'quite, quite blind', and she had agreed with him, adding: 'As an effing jellyfish, Charles, and twice as tasteless – but *what* a fascinating character.'

The fascinating character greeted her with a kiss on either cheek. She was obliged to stoop to accommodate him.

'Well, Sophronia,' he said, his English immaculate – Daddy had made enough money from one oil well to pack him off on the small change to Eton for his education – 'how delightful to see you again.' The rich, well-modulated tones emerging from this small, oddly dressed creature still managed to take her by surprise.

I really *don't* like the little bugger, Lord Sandhurst was thinking as he shook his hand. Don't like him at all. Poor Mumsy must be turning in her grave. Sandhurst's mother had been a lady of the old school, slightly more than wealthy, elegant, of immaculate taste and the finest of manners, who, in the absence of a father who had popped off to his maker after falling from his horse during a hunt when Sandhurst was quite small, had brought him up to mix only with the very best of society. Not that, as a teenager in the thirties, he had not drunk, gambled and fornicated with the dubious as well as the best behind her back. Colourful characters were a frequent source of amusement; this desert rat with his impertinent accent had served to amuse for no more than a brief spell. Unfortunately, his wife appeared to be besotted with him; and Sophronia wore the trousers.

There were no other British guests that evening. Strangely, considering his taste in general, Sulman was cultivating the Sandhursts. It amused him and inflated his ego to have titled and famous friends, and he particularly enjoyed the company of the regally beautiful Sophronia. The lady might be sixty but she was remarkably well preserved, knowledgeable and witty. The old fool was not such an old fool either – he could always be depended upon to tell amusing anecdotes at dinner about their experiences in various parts of the world. He also played a good game of backgammon, which Sulman enjoyed.

Despite her fascination with him – or perhaps because of it – Lady Sandhurst had decided that the sheikh was unbelievably weird, even perhaps quite mad. It was one thing to have bodyguards surrounding him when he went out and to have his ghastly house ringed with television cameras, but something else to repeat the arrangements within the asylum; for there were security cameras in every room and passageway. And everywhere one went – for the sheikh did encourage his guests to wander at will, delighting in showing off a villa which he seemed to imagine was a showcase of exquisite refinement – there were these dreadful, bulky hoodlums hanging around, lurking like thieves in the night about to mug one. Even at dinner.

It was the same story that evening.

The dining-room was long and narrow with green-and-gold, fleur-de-lis-patterned flock wallpaper and a banqueting table to seat fifty running almost its entire length. Tonight there was just a handful of people for dinner, most of them house guests, all of them, in Sandhurst's opinion, suspicious-looking. Yet a table along a whole wall groaned and sagged with food. There must have been enough to feed an entire Spanish hamlet – silver plate upon silver plate, heaped with many different varieties of cooked meat and fish, with rice and potatoes, with an inconceivable variety of vegetables – all those platters kept hot with a system of burners. An orchard of fruit, perfectly fresh, sat in crushed ice – oranges, bananas, apples, melons, pomegranates, lychees, mangroves, kiwi fruits, plums and damsons, figs and dates.

The menus were comprehensive, larger than those of many restaurants, their offerings served by eight, spotlessly jacketed waiters with white bow-ties. Three times during the meal a pair of white-aproned, tall-hatted chefs with black-and-white checked trousers came in to see that all was in order.

Outside each of the two, wide-open doors at either end of this feasting-room, all the way through dinner there leant against walls, idly chatting as their eyes disinterestedly wandered over the assembly, three bodyguards.

Sophronia and Charles Sandhurst, who in their time had graced the tables of some of the world's richest people, were once again impressed. There was not only a magnificent display of food, but everything they sampled was of the highest quality.

What annoyed Sandhurst was the obligation to drink bottled mineral water or soft drinks with one's food, though he did manage to sneak a healthy shot of vodka from his hip-flask into a glass of tonic water under cover of the tablecloth.

One did not question the sheikh about his

private life, the Sandhursts had discovered that during their first social evening with him. Such a transgression was greeted with a brief, expressionless silence followed by a change of subject. One waited for him to volunteer information. The fact that he was an arms dealer was very much a part of the public-rumour domain. But this was one taboo subject which he had never discussed with anyone other than those with whom he did business.

Sulman was at the head of the table, Sophronia to his left, world-weary nineteen-year-old Marian, uncomfortable on a sore rear end, to his right.

'Potatoes,' he suddenly said to Lady Sandhurst. 'Did I tell you that I trade worldwide in potatoes?'

She blinked at him from behind her no-nonsense spectacles. 'I've never actually heard a great deal about the potato market, curiously enough.'

'They came from South America originally, now they are grown throughout the world. There are something like eighteen thousand varieties of them. I have more or less cornered the market.'

He's taking the piss, thought Sophronia. 'Really,' she said – it sounded like 'rarely' – 'well, that's *most* interesting.'

'I deal in rice as well.' The sheikh swallowed a morsel of the tenderest of baby lamb with iced spring water. 'By the millions of tons.'

He *is* taking the piss, thought her ladyship. A dealer in the innocuous potato and harmless little grains of rice terrified for his skin? It made as much sense as gang warfare over strawberry jam.

'You've probably heard the gossip about me being an arms trader?'

Her ears pricked up. First time he had mentioned *that* little number. 'No, actually,' she lied. 'Well, perhaps a little whisper here or there.'

'You've heard. But I'm not offended. Were I – and I'm not – I shouldn't be ashamed of it. Business, after all, is only business. If men want to kill one another then somebody has to supply them with the wherewithal.' He smiled. It was not a smile to cheer one's soul; the slitty mouth with its damp lips obeyed the rules but his eyes failed to comply.

Marian's smile was brittle, too. Potatoes, you dirty git, she was thinking, I'd like to stuff them one by one up your nether regions until you burst.

'Well, well. Potatoes and rice, then. How entralling,' chirruped Sophronia.

Bullshit, more like, thought Lord Sandhurst, eyeing his host with distaste. He, too, managed to conceal his true feelings behind a lying smile.

12

'It's not at all easy, so it isn't,' said Guy Keegan. He winced, and gingerly touched his left shoulder; he had been sunburnt the day before. Like the idiot he was, he told himself, he had left his towel draped over his right shoulder for the entire one and a half hours he spent wandering in the vicinity of Casa al-Riyadh, and his left had turned raw.

'Life is difficult. It makes it that much more interesting,' retorted Forbes. He downed a pre-lunch Tío Pepe and ordered another one.

'Life is nice and simple in my little shop in Parsons Green, thanks a bundle. That's the way I prefer it.' As he poured some cold draught San Miguel down his throat, Keegan appeared to be chomping on the glass. 'One lump of lead in the belly is enough in anyone's lifetime.'

'You can do the job, right?'

'*It* can be done, to be sure.' He stressed the word 'it'.

'You're under orders, remember? We're supposed to be one smooth unit. And you're responsible for the telephone tap, Guy. Nobody else.'

'Heaven help me.'

Forbes glanced around the room, thinking. They were occupying the lavishly decorated Marbella Club bar, putting the lavish prices on Hammid Mullah's bill. There were only a handful of people there, as most of the guests were around the pool or down at the beach. Alone at the corner of the bar, on a stool, was sitting an attractive redhead in a miniskirt which almost revealed her knickers. Forbes's eyes met hers for an instant to discover a question mark in their cat-like green. Hooker, he thought; whores had always held a certain fascination for him, though he had never in his life paid for one. His eyes travelled over her legs then back to the Irishman.

'We'll need to work out some sort of a diversion for you. How much time will you need?'

'Ten, fifteen minutes at least. Time enough to get picked off like a sitting duck, even if I do it in the dead of night.'

Tristram MacDowell entered the bar and joined them. He had been on surveillance duty near Sulman's villa. Forbes was rotating his men to keep watch there and to shadow the sheikh's convoy. He had decided that they were going to have to snatch the man from his Merc and a plan of attack was shaping up in his mind though as yet he remained uncertain as to where this would take place.

As the tall Scot ordered a beer he said to the two men: 'He paid a visit to my movie-star compatriot's house.'

'Did he now?' A second visit to James Kennedy's place. Tucked away as it was among a maze of little, leafy lanes close to the beach, it was already one of the possible locations for the kidnapping in Forbes's mind.

'Sure, and you should have taken up acting yourself, Tristram. You've the looks of Charles Laughton and Boris Karloff rolled into one, so you do,' said Keegan through a twisted grin.

'And you'll have the face of a squashed tomato if you don't shut it.' But MacDowell was smiling as he sipped his beer. It was great to be back in action. His beady eye, delighted to be at rest from constantly contemplating his little-loved, dowdy wife, fell on the whore – where it remained. She sent him the same explicit signal as she had telegraphed to Forbes.

'Top of her class, feller,' said Forbes. 'She's sitting on pure gold.'

'I'm a prospector.' The Scot still had not taken his eyes from the woman. Slowly, he said: 'Do you have anything for me to do right now?'

'You've covered your ground for the day.'

He swallowed his beer rapidly, his gaze roving again over the hooker's body. 'Then, to hell with the expense, I'm gonna do *her*.' He moved in. She welcomed him with metaphorically open arms.

'Well, how do you like that now?' asked Keegan.

'I like it a lot. But I prefer my wife. And she's free.'

'There's no such animal as a free wife. Did you not find that out yet?'

Forbes remembered the last Valentino dress. 'You know something? You're dead bloody right.' It had been the colour of a London bus. The recollection struck a chord in his mind. A London bus. He thought it over.

MacDowell was deep in earnest conversation with the redhead. 'He's a Scottish tightwad,' said Keegan. 'He'll be knocking her price down, so he will.'

Forbes ignored the comment. 'You know something, Guy? You won't tap that phone at night. You'll do it in broad daylight.'

'The hell I will.'

'You'll have your fifteen minutes. A little more, if you need it.'

Keegan gaped at him as if he had suddenly turned bright green. But then he interpreted that special look in Forbes's eyes; he had seen it before. He smiled. 'Tell me how, boss,' he said.

Twenty minutes later, with Keegan departed to find Roldán and take him shopping, Leila joined her husband in the bar to go off for lunch. She did not particularly fancy a drink but as Forbes finished his and was about to ask for the tab to sign, he noticed two interesting individuals coming in.

'Two more Tío Pepes,' he said to the barman.

'I thought we were going to eat?' said Leila. 'I'm peckish.'

'It can wait.'

She saw the way he was looking at the elderly couple who were propping their well-clad behinds on stools on the other side of the curve of the bar. 'Who are they?'

'You're about to find out.'

As Lord Sandhurst ordered a Stolichnaya and tonic for himself and a glass of white wine for his wife, Forbes called out breezily: 'Hello, there.'

They both stared at him. Lady Sandhurst blinked and smiled weakly; her husband frowned and said: 'Do we know you, old boy?'

'We met very briefly,' said Forbes, his mind racing. 'At the baroness's, wasn't it? Aren't you Lord and Lady Sandhurst?' He figured there were probably enough baronesses scattered around the coast to pack a royal garden party, so it was not a bad stab.

'Terry's, was it?' trilled Sophronia.

'Right.' Forbes nodded at their glasses. 'Let me put those on my bill.'

'Frightfully kind of you, Mr . . . er . . . ?' said Lady Sandhurst.

More lightning thinking as he saw the Scot leaving the bar for his expensive roll in the hay. 'Scott,' he told her. 'Stephen Scott.'

Lord Sandhurst invited them across. 'This is my wife, Leila,' said Forbes.

Wife? Fat chance, thought Sophronia – wrong for a change – taking Leila's hand in her heavily ringed one, she's your little bit on the side sneaked down to sunny Marbella for a naughty.

'I'm afraid I don't remember you too clearly, old boy,' said Sandhurst. 'Down here on holiday, are you?'

'I'm researching a novel.'

Now what's the devious sod up to? thought Leila, All of a sudden he's a writer. Then she recalled that he had, in fact, long ago had aspirations in that direction. He had made, so he thought, a quite passable effort at a thriller; the neatly elastic-banded bunch of rejection slips in his desk drawer indicated a rather different professional opinion.

'How fascinating,' said Lady Sandhurst. 'Should I know your name, or do you have a pen-name?' Her gold bangles jangled as she picked up her glass of wine and swept it towards her heavily painted lips.

'You probably wouldn't have heard of me,' Forbes told her, lying through his teeth, not quite sure why his subconscious mind was urging him along in this direction. 'I've only had one or two reviews. The second book's due out shortly and right now I'm working on the third.'

'What is it – sex?' asked his lordship hopefully.

'Suspense.'

What you're putting me in, thought Leila.

'What's it called? The one that's just out? We'll have to keep an eye out for it when we're in London. It is being published in England, I take it?'

'England, yes. And the States, with any luck. *The Suicide Man.*'

Leila just avoided spluttering into her Tío Pepe.

Lord Sandhurst had been pouring vodka tonic down his noble, leathery-skinned throat as if quenching a monumental thirst. The glass hovered. The discreet little, flawless diamond on his square-ended pinkie caught the light and sharded it. 'Macabre sort of title, isn't it, old man?'

'I suppose it is, yes. My publisher thinks it will shift books.' Forbes had already warmed to his new role and was falling effortlessly into it, having a little fun.

'I think it's rather a *good* title, Charles,' opined Sophronia. She cackled. 'Except that one can't be a suicide man more than once, can one, if you see what I mean?'

Forbes pulled his chummy, sixth-form grin, the one his salesman self was well aware everyone liked. 'There won't be a sequel, Lady Sandhurst.'

She cackled again.

'I'll let you have a copy as soon as it's published. I'd love to know what you and your husband think of it.'

'Well, thank you.' She smiled approvingly at him. 'It's Sophronia, actually. Sophronia and Charles.' She was already beginning to like this honest-faced, ruggedly handsome man. Wasn't sure about the tart, though. She hadn't uttered a word since joining them – just stood there prettily sipping her drink like the dumb little idiot she no doubt was.

Having listened to Forbes in silence for the past five minutes, Leila was only just coming out of a mild case of shock. What on earth did he think he was up to with his three books and his research and his reviews, not to mention his published in the States with any luck? There were times when he completely bemused her, although on the other hand, that was one of his attractions.

By the time the little party broke up, Leila having finally joined in the conversation and thereby demonstrated to Sophronia that she was far from the dumb chick she had supposed, the four were on jolly, buddy-buddy terms.

'What on earth was that incredible heap of shit about?' Leila asked Forbes as the two of them sat down for lunch under a Chinese-lantern-festooned tree close to a cage teaming with brilliantly coloured tropical birds in the club's restaurant garden. 'It was just about the biggest bunch of Tartuffery I've ever heard from you.'

'Of what?'

'Tartuffery. I read it in a magazine this morning. Didn't understand it either. I looked it up. Bullshit.'

'I wrote a book, did I not? It was OK; it should have been published. I've read worse. Jeffrey Archer, for example.'

'But why the whole string of lies?'

He was scanning the menu. Lately he needed glasses for this, which did not please him. 'You know, I'm not even sure myself.'

'Going round the twist, are we?'

'Who knows?' He put the menu down and raised a hand for the waiter. 'You don't realize who the Sandhursts are, do you? I mean in relation to our particular little bit of business?'

'Should I?'

138

He told her. Then he said: 'I have a hunch they might come in useful somewhere along this rocky road. I thought it best to make a favourable impression on them. So what do I tell them? The truth?'

'Hardly, darling. Christ.'

'Exactly. I could have volunteered no information at all – and that class of people are far too well bred to ask. But I wanted to interest them. My head kinda pushed me into that, ah, Tartuffery, was it? A good ploy, as it happens. Worked a dream.'

'Come around any time you like for lunch, *do*, Stephen,' Lady Sandhurst had said warmly. She had given him her telephone number.

A good ploy indeed. Better than Forbes, aka Scott, could have possibly imagined. But that was going to be for much later.

13

Albert Tidy's gnarled fingers, with their little clumps of wiry, salt-and-pepper hair, tightened on the steering wheel of his Fiesta. Headlights. From where he was parked with his own lights off, at the entrance to the slip-road which brought traffic on and off the N340, the turret of Casa al-Riyadh looked like that of a doll's house. Down below, the powerful beams of the stretch Cadillac knifed into the darkness as the huge car pulled on to the lane and rolled slowly towards the pine wood. The gates remained open but there was no other car throwing light on to the tarmac in front.

In the Cadillac six armed men peered through the black, bulletproof windows, their eyes probing the trees. The headlights washed through the wood, painting it a ghostly white against a backdrop of sharp-edged, slowly moving shadows, picking out every blade of grass, the lilacs, the rubbish.

Sulman's heavies did not expect to find an

ambush party. Privately they considered the boss's normal precautions – never mind the latest ones – way over the top. They carried them out anyway. Who gives a shit? – he pays us by the sackful, they reasoned. There was nobody lying in wait. But there was, as very occasionally happened along that lonely part of the coast at night, a car parked off the road among the trees, in darkness.

The young man and girl on the rear seat of the car were too carried away to immediately react to the lights invading their mobile bedroom. Two of the sheikh's bodyguards, hands inside their jackets, were leering through the back window before the couple realized it.

The girl's flaxen head bobbed up from the boy's crotch. She gaped in embarrassed surprise at the two shadowy figures bending down, staring at them. As her boyfriend dragged his shirt tail over his erection and snatched at his underpants, she grabbed for her knee-hugging knickers, choking back a scream.

The men laughed. 'Have one for me,' muttered one of them, and they went back to the Cadillac. Inside, he spoke briefly into his walkie-talkie. 'All clear, sir,' he said.

Tidy had his binoculars to his eyes as the Mercedes 280SL left, its protective big brother the 600 close on its little red tail with its lights on dim. He followed the progreess of the two cars as they caught up with the first and the three of them rolled through the wood.

The boy hooked a thumb into the waistband of the girl's panties and tried to pull them back down her bare legs. She stopped him.

'No,' she said, in Spanish. 'For God's sake, no.'

'But they've gone, Ana,' he protested. 'Don't leave me like this.'

'Find somewhere else, idiot.'

Tidy switched on his engine, then his sidelights, as the Arab procession began to pull out on to the highway, in the direction of Marbella. It had been a mistake to turn on his lights that quickly. A pair of hawk eyes narrowed as they stared backwards from the big Mercedes.

As the Merc moved into the night-time traffic Tidy accelerated down the slip-road. He spotted the lights of the lovers' car as it left the wood. What the fuck is this? he thought. He followed them at a discreet distance out on to the highway, where he saw that a girl's head was leaning on a boy's shoulder. Overtaking their battered Renault, he closed in to within two hundred metres of the Arabs and sat there.

Hawk-eye was on to him. 'There's a chance we're being tailed,' he said. 'That white Fiesta behind us was parked in the slip-road. Now it's sitting on our arse.'

None of the other three heads in the 600 moved around. Hawk-eye faced the front and the driver watched in a rear-view mirror big enough to afford him not just a panorama of the road behind but also of the surrounding countryside.

'Step on it a bit,' said the driver into his walkie-talkie to the driver of the Cadillac. The procession increased its speed to a hundred and twenty kilometres per hour. Tidy stayed with it. 'Drop down to a hundred.' Tidy slowed, with no more thought in his head than that Arabs were bloody erratic drivers. 'He's on our tail, all right.'

There was a conference between the two escort cars and the boss. They were making for a restaurant in Puerto Banús. Sulman instructed them that when they reached Guadalmina Baja, an urbanization just before San Pedro, they should leave the highway and navigate the maze of roads down towards the beach there. 'Make absolutely sure,' he told them. 'If you're right I'll teach the swine.'

Tidy followed them, never quite letting them out of his sight as they drove through scruffy fields dotted with expensive houses – this was a rich-man's area which had never managed to get its act together infrastructure-wise, badly maintained, its roads crumbling, its street lamps broken.

Nearing the beach, as the Cadillac passed a large house with a two-metre-high privet hedge around it and a junction at the corner of the hedge Sulman peered over his skinny shoulder; the son of a bitch was a hundred and fifty metres behind. The sheikh was sick to his stomach of whatever was going on. He was also running scared, holding, as he did, his unprecious life only a little less in esteem than that of his king.

'Left turn ahead. Block the road,' he ordered. 'Kill the whoreson.'

As one by one the cars veered around the corner and out of sight, Tidy hit the accelerator. He slowed to corner, but he took it fast enough for his tyres to squeal. Straightening, he slammed on his brakes. The big Merc was blocking the road, and three heavies had spilled from it and were pointing in his direction the kind of hardware he preferred to be on the other end of. It was the week of the fair and Tidy had just been set up as a shooting gallery.

He jammed his gear-stick into reverse – a futile action. The Arabs opened fire with silenced Smith & Wesson 459s. A bullet shattered his windscreen and tore through his shoulder; another ripped through his lung. A third plopped almost dead centre into his forehead, rearranging his grey matter and punching a handful of it over the rear seat of the Fiesta.

Albert Tidy was tidy no more.

14

The sheikh and the Cadillac had gone. There was nobody else around. The killers quickly checked the inside of the Fiesta and went through Tidy's pockets. He was carrying no weapon – as far as they were concerned that was, but he had up his sleeve one or two nasty little tricks with a sharpened nail-file which his ghost would no doubt have taken great pleasure in inflicting on them at that moment. The binoculars sitting on the passenger seat told their own story, and he had on his person a document which, monitored through certain channels, should give them considerably more information about him. His British passport. They took just the little red book and sped off.

Stephen Forbes was unaware that anything was amiss until his team arrived for their morning meeting at Casa Puck. As usual they arrived individually at prearranged five-minute intervals, but Tidy failed to fit into his slot. Already, by ten thirty-five, Forbes had reason for concern. The discipline of split-second timing was essential in his team and in this respect, like the rest of the men, the Brummie was a perfectionist. It was inconceivable that he had overslept, but just in case Forbes had Leila put in a call to his room at the Guadalpín Hotel.

Keegan reported having got together his little bag of tricks for his assault on Casa al-Riyadh's telephone line and Roldán had been successful in setting up Forbes's master plan concerning this; they would between them be putting it into action at midday.

At five to eleven Hammid Mullah showed up, bringing with him accessories vital to Forbes's as yet unscheduled snatch of the sheikh. There was a false passport, freshly issued through the competent authority in Kuwait. And he carried a cumbersome cardboard box, secured with string.

'What the hell are these?' asked Forbes, opening the box and peering at the hardware neatly packed inside in cotton wool, as Leila remembered to tune into the local English-language radio station for the eleven o'clock news.

Someone with a keener sense of humour than the accountant might have said something like 'toffee-apples', but he merely grunted: 'Guns – what else?'

Forbes took one out. 'Where in the name of God did your embassy get hold of these?'

'That shooter's got slitty eyes, ain't it?' observed Freddie Fraser.

'You're right. They're 9mm Type 59 Chinese pistols,' said Forbes, turning it over, examining it. 'Amazing.'

'Aren't they any good?' asked Mullah.

Johnnie Johnson put his oar in. 'Providing you don't actually want to shoot someone. They have a wonderful reputation for jamming.'

'The Kuwaiti Embassy isn't an arsenal,' said Mullah huffily. 'Neither is it the Department of War.'

'They'll do at a pinch.' Forbes was taking the guns out one by one. 'Thoroughly oiled, they shouldn't jam. The only place our little yellow friends know to put grease is on their hair. In any case, if all goes to plan we won't be firing them.' He glanced at Mullah. 'Silencers. Where are the silencers?'

'You didn't ask for any.'

'Christ, I did.' But, no, Christ, I didn't, thought Forbes. I've got to watch myself, I'm slipping.

'I'm sorry, Mr Forbes, you didn't. I wrote it down. I don't make mistakes.' He produced a notepad and briefly scanned a page. 'Nothing about silencers. In any case, why would you be wanting them if you don't think there'll be any shooting?'

Forbes glared at him. 'Silencers? *Please*?' he growled. 'Like, within twenty-four hours?'

'Sssshhhh! Quiet everybody. Listen to this.' Excited, Leila turned the radio right up.

It was news of Albert Tidy's murder. The police had taken his name from the car-hire papers. Someone from a nearby house had been just going out to walk the dog and had been almost knocked down in the street by a big, black, speeding Mercedes. He had discovered the bloody killing. Police suspected it was either a gangland murder involving drug dealers or a Mafia-type settling of accounts; it was common knowledge that there was a British criminal element well established on the coast, though the small bunch of known villains wanted back in Blighty kept their noses clean.

They were all stunned. Poor Albert. One stiff already and they hadn't even gone into action.

'Fuck,' said Forbes quietly.

Keegan looked as if he was going to cry. 'He was a fine man, to be sure.'

'Not fine enough to stay out of the way of a bullet. The poor sod made some stupid mistake or other.' Forbes looked hard at each of them. 'It's the toughest lesson we can learn. We're not dealing with a kids' playgroup.'

Hammid Mullah was looking pensive. Forbes stared daggers at him; he could almost see the man's brain busily calculating. 'Not a chance, pal,' he told him. 'Don't even think about it. Tidy's fifteen grand goes to his old lady.'

Mullah left, followed by Freddie Fraser and MacDowell, who each took a gun with them. Then Roldán and Keegan left to get on with their tricky business. Forbes followed them. He had to settle the fee due to the driver of the vehicle essential to their plan. At the door he paused to say: 'Stick around for a while if you like, Johnnie. Keep Leila company. I've a couple of other things to do. Doubt if I'll be back before two.' It was eleven thirty-five.

'Keep Leila company.' Dangerous words. Forbes might be Johnnie's boss and a buddy, but crumpet ruled his life. His clothes-penetrating gaze invaded Leila as the door closed. Not that there was much clothing to see through. She was barefoot, her toenails painted the same shade of mauve as her fingernails. She had on tiny white shorts, tight as skin, and a blue cotton blouse which her breasts thrust saucily at him, exhibiting cleavage and the top edges of a skimpy, lacy, white bra.

What was Steve up to? Was he throwing Leila at him? Was he running out of steam and needing her serviced? Wickedly disloyal thoughts, he knew, but lovely women – especially this one with her perfect little body, her sultry eyes and thick, shiny hair cascading across those slender shoulders – tended to inspire a flood of them.

'Drink?' muttered Leila.

She found herself distinctly uncomfortable to be unexpectedly left alone with this attractive, talented specimen of hunky manhood. The last time at his cottage in Ross-on-Wye it had been difficult enough for her to repel his repeated advances; the temptation to succumb had been strong. Him and his Clark Gable grin and his oozing male potency. Each time he had visited Casa Puck his frequent, plainly sexual glances had jolted her libido. Now here they were, thrown together by her idiot husband – and this wasn't the West Country; it was sun, sex and sangria, and the temperature was hovering in the eighties. She was always randier in hot weather. Shit, Stephen knew that. He must have noticed the way Johnnie was always looking at her.

Stephen shouldn't do this to her. She loved him dearly, but she was young, very aware of the effect she had on other men – particularly Johnnie – and this awareness in itself contrived to turn her on. Stephen shouldn't do it.

While she poured gin into two glasses her back seemed to be crackling like the ice cubes as she felt his eyes boring into it. She added tonic, trying to beat down the cloud of butterflies rising in her belly.

'Well,' he said, 'cheers.' He clinked his glass against hers. 'Here's to us.'

And, damn him, he was wearing tight designer jeans with a plain white T-shirt through which his pectorals bulged. 'What do you mean, to us?'

His eyes locked on hers. 'To the team. To success. What else?'

The bloody liar. 'Yes.'

She gulped down her drink. The Gordon's seemed to hit her tight little belly with more impact than usual.

'You know something, Leila? You are one total knockout. Steve or no Steve, I can't trust myself with you.'

She walked nervously out on to the terrace. And I can't trust myself with you. 'Then why don't you piss off?' she threw over her shoulder.

Not when there was a chance of this top-quality nooky. He followed her outside, randy eyes hooking greedily into her perfect, tightly out-lined buttocks. 'That's not what I call friendly.'

She took a very deep breath, letting it out slowly as she turned to face him. She gulped more gin and tonic; two-thirds of the highball glass was already inside her, an indication of her tension.

'Look, Johnnie,' she said, struggling to keep her voice firm and steady, her eyes dancing all over his face but scared to meet his again, 'we've been through all this before. Leave it out, will you?'

He grinned that devastating grin. 'You fancy me,' he said bluntly. He knew he was dead bloody right. Women were his speciality, and the signs were written all over her. She fancied him for sure.

She found no sharp reply. Instead she bit her bottom lip. Her gaze retreated to his feet. Shit, get your arse back here this minute, Stephen, she was thinking. Get me out of this. Get us *both* out of this.

Johnnie closed in on her to tilt her chin up with the rim of his glass. 'Steve doesn't have to know,' he said, confidence mounting by the second, particularly since she had failed to deny his challenge. 'This is strictly between you, me and the bed.'

She gasped. 'Bastard.'

'That's the spirit, baby.' Christ, he couldn't remember when he had last wanted a woman as much as he wanted Leila. He would donate half his fee to Battersea Dirty Dogs Home to get into those delectable knickers.

Her belly was churning. She was going weak at the knees. 'You'd better leave,' she managed to mumble. 'Right now, there's a good boy.'

Putting his barely touched glass down carefully on a coffee table as she swigged the last in hers with a sort of desperation, he quietly asked: 'Or what, Leila?'

'Sling your fucking hook,' she muttered.

'Language, language.' Hearing that word spilling from her pretty lips inflamed him even further.

It had much the same impact on her. She almost exclusively reserved it for sex, she had certainly never used it in front of anybody but her husband since they were married. Throwing it at Johnnie like that seemed to crystallize her emotions.

It was inevitable. Seconds later she was in his arms, her lips mashing into his in a frenzy of passion, crotch thrusting against his steely-muscled thigh. Her head was spinning with more than the effect of the hastily downed triple Gordon's as he dragged her inside the bungalow and pulled her down with him on to a leather sofa, his hands hungrily, feverishly, travelling all over her.

He practically ripped open her blouse, unclipped the hooks joining her bra cups, freed her breasts and closed his mouth on them.

What happened next was perhaps just as inevitable as the onset of this sexual threshing. With Johnnie sucking on her nipple and his hand fumbling between her legs as the other unzipped his jeans, a great wave of guilt engulfed Leila.

Panting with desire, she nevertheless metamorphosed into a furiously spitting little tiger.

Grabbing him by the hair, she dragged Johnnie's face off her breasts. She ripped his hand from her crotch and delivered an angry, stinging crack of a slap to his cheek. She struggled to her feet, pointing with a trembling finger towards the door.

'Get out!' Get out of here!' she screamed, flushed with sexual passion and rage. 'Out. Out.' And again she bellowed: '*Out!*'

He stared at her as if she had gone raving mad. 'What the fu . . . ?'

'You dirty bastard. Go. Leave.' She was shaking from head to foot. 'Right now, or I'll tell Stephen and he'll have your balls.' She screamed the last word.

Johnnie's turn to get angry. He pushed himself to his feet and zipped up his fly. 'Why, you crazy little bitch,' he snarled at her. 'You think you can do this to a man and get away with it? I've killed for less.'

'You did it to yourself,' she spat through closed teeth. It's your bloody fault, not mine. You should have left me alone, you bastard. I'm Stephen's wife. Stephen, your so-called friend. Your boss. Now piss off.'

Johnnie, anger seeping into every bone in his body, humiliated, defeated, stormed to the door, where he turned on Leila, his eyes blazing fire. 'I'm going, bitch,' he snarled, wagging his finger at her. 'But I'm going to *have* you, Leila. One day I'm going to screw your nutty brains out.' And he was gone, slamming the door hard enough to rattle the pictures.

Leila collapsed on the sofa, where she did something she had not done in years. She sobbed her heart out.

15

The twenty-seven-year-old, one-time London Transport double-decker bus appeared as out of place lumbering around the streets of Marbella as would a rhino grazing on Hampstead Heath. But it was an attention-grabber which gaily performed a duty unheard of in its London days. Plastered with colourful advertisements, it was driven every day around the town and the surrounding urbanizations broadcasting music over loudspeakers – curiously mixing flamenco with rock and roll.

At twelve-fifteen that morning the bus was off its customary route. In a lay-by on the N340, a kilometre and a half from Casa al-Riyadh, its speakers temporarily silenced, it was being doctored – under the attentive eye of Luis Roldán – by its heavily suborned Spanish driver. The driver was crouching in front of the big, black radiator. Its tap was open and rusty-coloured water was pouring out into the gutter.

Meanwhile Guy Keegan, wearing dark-green

swimming shorts and a black T-shirt, and carrying a beach bag containing gear most essential,
had been dropped off by taxi on the other side
of the wood which fronted the sheikh's villa and
was making his way cautiously through the trees,
staying under cover.

The last drops of water dripped from the
radiator.

'It won't be going very far like this,' pointed
out the driver, unnecessarily, in Spanish.

Roldán ran a hand over the top of his
Brylcreemed head; he had the habit of need-
lessly slicking back hair which already clung to
his pate like a fresh coat of pitch on a road.
He strode around to the open entrance to the
bus and produced an unopened plastic bottle
of Lanjerón mineral water from where once the
conductor used to stow his ticket machine. He
took the bottle to the driver, stripping the plastic
seal from its neck as he went.

'Close the tap,' said Roldán. 'Empty this in the
radiator.'

'It won't go very far with one shit litre of water,
either,' protested the driver.

'That's the general idea.'

'But this is madness, no? You are ruining
my bus.'

Roldán showed the man the envelope which
contained the other half of the hundred thousand

pesetas Forbes was paying him for an hour or so's hire of the ancient vehicle. 'We almost bought the whore-bus.'

The driver shrugged; so what, it was not his property in any case – he was just paid to chauffeur it around. If the engine blew up it could be repaired. He did as was asked.

Keegan was lurking behind a fat pine tree on the eastern edge of the wood, its trunk between himself and Casa al-Riyadh, as the bus grumbled through the wood with its radiator wheezing and steaming. As his eyes followed its progress, his pulse began to quicken in excitement.

'What in the name of Allah?' spluttered one of the two of Sulman's bodyguards who were playing backgammon while manning the bank of security monitors within the house.

The music of the Beatles warbling 'Lady Madonna' had suddenly invaded the room. As the men's eyes flickered over the screens, garish advertising began rolling from right to left in front of the camera covering the right-hand front gate, past it, and hit the one atop the left-hand gatepost.

'Commercials?' exclaimed the bemused body-guard, thinking for a moment that somehow the system had hooked into satellite TV.

The ads stopped rolling. Old Vic's Disco, The

Best in Town, was spread in red and gold across the left-hand gate screen.

The Arabs abandoned their game and barged from the room.

Keegan, a set of brand-new tree-climbing spikes attached to the soles of his trainers, a roll of telephone wire over his shoulder, was shinning up the four-metre-high pole which was one of the series taking Casa al-Riyadh's telephone line to the highway from where it went underground into the general system. His bag was less than ten metres away from him. It sat behind the pine tree, at the edge of the wood, into which he had already speedily rubber-hammered, under cover of the raucous music from the bus, several black-painted climbing pegs. On reaching the wire, he began to scrape a section of it clean in order to make a perfect connection.

The gate within the belly of one of the bronze elephants slammed open. The bodyguards found themselves confronted with a side of the parked bus, less than half a metre from their noses, as the blaring music switched from Beatles to Chiquetete singing 'Sevilla Sin Tu Amor'. Hands within their bulging shirts, they squeezed between the bus and the cypress hedge to where the driver and Roldán had the bus's bonnet up and were staring mournfully at the boiling radiator.

'Get this heap away from our gates, will you,

man?' shouted one of the heavies in English. 'It's blocking them.'

Roldán shrugged and replied in English: 'As you can see, señor, this bus, it is out of water. These things happen.'

'Then don't just stand there. Put some fucking water *in* it.'

'But to remove the little hat now, this is dangerous, do you understand? She throw steam in our faces. We burn. We must wait.'

Roldán suddenly realized that, while Keegan may be off the security camera, some distance away and no bigger than a bird from there, he was within the men's field of vision. The Colombian shoved his way past the men, making for the open elephant's belly. 'You must have a hose in your garden, no?' he said. 'We wait, but meanwhile I get this. We carry no water.'

'Oi!' exclaimed one of the men as they both ran after him. Roldán's arm was grabbed as he lifted a foot to step through the gate.

'With no water, this bus it no move.'

'What is the bloody bus doing here anyway?'

'Our boss, he wants that we drive on every road. Every person from Fuengirola to Estepona, he must see the publicity.'

'Our boss has the only house on this road. And *our* boss has no need of *your* boss's ridiculous bus.' The Arab raised his hands to his ears. 'For fuck's sake, turn that racket off.'

Silence returned to the vicinity. Keegan, his tapping wire firmly clipped to Sulman's telephone line, made his way down the pole. Every half metre, using a staple gun, he attached his wire to the side of the pole away from the villa. On reaching the ground, he crouched low and began to scrape a rut in the loamy earth with a wide chisel, burying the wire and covering it up as he backed towards his tree.

Irritated but unsuspicious, the bodyguards disappeared to fetch water. Roldán went around to the front of the bus, from where he noticed with relief that the tiny figure of Keegan had almost reached the trees. The bus driver, who understood no English, was gloomily watching his radiator as the bubbling noise within began to calm. Not the brightest of the bright, he had formed in his mind no association between the fact that the bus had been brought to a halt on Roldán's instructions precisely in front of a security camera and that that might have been to deliberately block it.

'I do not understand,' said the driver helplessly. 'Why are you doing such a crazy thing?'

'Let's say it's a sort of a game. I like mucking people about.'

'You like mucking people about? Oh.'

The Arabs reappeared, one of them carrying a full, red plastic watering-can. Roldán saw that Keegan had made it to the cover of the wood. The driver took hold of the radiator cap with an oily rag and began to gingerly unscrew it.

'This is not enough water,' he said. 'Better use the hose.'

'So we'll have them fetch another bucket.'

The compressed steam in the radiator hissed threateningly out as the cap came off. The Spaniard leapt wildly away from it with a screech of alarm; Roldán guffawed.

Keegan was up his tree among dense foliage, his beach bag slung over his shoulder. He had reached a place where three sturdy branches forked; it was not perfection, but it would have to do. From the bag he produced some rope netting with which he rigged a makeshift hammock affair in which to make himself as comfortable as possible.

Five minutes later as the bus's engine growled into life and the peace of the copse was once again disturbed by raucous, tinny flamenco music, Keegan was making the final connections of his hand-set eavesdropping equipment to the wire attached at its other end to Sulman's line. Settling down on his hammock, his back resting against a branch, his eyes on the progress of the brightly coloured bus, he put the receiver to his ear.

Keegan smiled in immense satisfaction. There were voices on the line. He had no way of knowing, because they were conversing in Arabic, but one of them was that of Sheikh Yasser Sulman himself. The sheikh was negotiating the clandestine transport of a further massive delivery of arms to Iraq, with Saddam Hussein's brother.

16

Forbes called a halt to the visual surveillance. He had the well-hidden telephone tap and every day he appointed a different man to climb up the tree and listen from dawn to dusk. It was an uncomfortable, tiresome vigil but the mercenaries had been through far worse in thoroughly inclement conditions and in far greater danger. They each took their turn cheerfully enough. Forbes could have rotated them on a half-day basis, but he wanted as little movement as was necessary in the wood.

He was almost ready to go into action. All he was waiting for now was a definite indication, comfortably in advance, that Sulman was planning to visit any one of three particular houses. For each of the luxury villas he had a separate, carefully worked-out plan of attack involving a particularly skilful and courageous act of daring performed by the man who was still scheming about how to have his evil way with Leila: Johnnie Johnson.

The three houses of the rich offered different, excellent opportunities for ambush. One, the closest to Sulman's residence, was that of the Baroness von Pantz, which, curiously enough, had an abandoned urbanization infrastructure similar to that near the sheikh's villa but dating back only a few years. Visitors were obliged to drive through it to gain access to the house and, apart from those and house guests and servants, hardly anyone used it.

The second was that of the actor James Kennedy. Surrounded as it was with narrow, high-treed lanes, unlit at night and with little traffic, it could not have suited the purpose better.

From one of the small roads surrounding the enormous villa presenting the third opportunity there had already been a kidnapping of worldwide notoriety, eight years previously. The property belonged to Raymond Nakachian, one-time London nightclub and casino owner turned international businessman, completely bald-headed, charismatic and married to pop-opera star Kimera.

Melodie, their daughter, after whom the house was named, was just six years old at the time. She was leaving for school, driven by Nakachian's son and his wife early one Monday morning. They were ambushed close to the villa – on a hillside on the other side of the N340 from the sea – and the little girl had been snatched away by a gang later discovered to have been French but for one Spaniard. She was kept in miserable conditions for twelve days, shifted from one location to another in a golf bag while her half-crazed father and the police hunted up and down the coast for her.

The gang had initially demanded $13 million in various currencies. Over the days this sum was gradually whittled down by Nakachian. Finally, no ransom was paid because the police carried out a brilliant operation, capturing most of the gang and rescuing Melodie. Indeed so fine had been their performance that they continued to hold a celebratory dinner with the Nakachian family every year to commemorate the date of the rescue: 20 November 1987.

Sulman was a friend of Raymond Nakachian. Since Forbes's surveillance had been in place, the entrepreneur had visited the sheikh once and Sulman had twice dined at Casa Melodie. Forbes had dug out old newspaper reports of the kidnapping and carefully studied its location. He could see no reason why the same lonely spot should not be used again for the abduction of Yasser Sulman.

17

In the event, the ambush was not to take place outside Casa Melodie. It was a few days later, all the men had done their day's stint up the pine tree and it was Tristram MacDowell, on his second turn in the 'nest', who picked up the information they were all waiting for.

'There can be no mistake?' Forbes asked him during the following morning's meeting. It was a Friday.

'It was him all right,' said the Scot. 'He announced himself on the phone, asked to speak to the sheikh. Besides, I couldn't mistake that voice. Sulman's going for dinner, he's to be the only guest and he's leaving early because Kennedy's off in the morning for the start of a new picture.'

'So. Tonight. What time is he due to arrive? You heard?'

'Aye. About nine.'

It was perfect: no more visitors, which meant no other cars leaving the star's villa at the same time to get in their hair. Having learnt a great deal about the sheikh's habits and knowing that it was in any case to be an early night, Forbes calculated that Sulman would be leaving between eleven and midnight. At that time of night it was unlikely there would be any other traffic in that lonely neck of the woods.

'You're a man short, and there's a shooter to spare,' said Leila when she and Forbes were alone together.

'Guns, Leila. They're called *guns*.'

'Christ, you use the word often enough.'

'It would please me if sometimes you'd . . .' He took her in his arms without finishing the sentence. 'Hell, I'll never educate you.'

'I'm a very educated chick.'

'No.' He smiled down at her and kissed the tip of her nose.

She snuggled into him, trying to forget Johnnie's lingering, steamy departing look which had almost succeeded in ripping its way into her soul. 'Yes I am.'

'The no was to your coming along tonight.'

'You're short-handed. There's ten of them and only six of you. Anyway, I want to be with you.'

'We have the advantage of surprise.'

'And they have the advantage of a Cadi with black windows.' Breaking away from Forbes, she stalked to the open terrace windows to stare moodily at the jacaranda tree. When she turned to face him her arms were firmly crossed over her cream halter top. He was pouring himself a beer. 'You're drinking early,' she said curtly.

'Maybe.' He took a slug of the foamy lager. She was going to be difficult – he could tell by the way she was standing.

'Stephen, I'm deadly serious. You're going to want me to wait here for you until you get back. I've got no nerves when it comes to action, you know that. But you leave me sitting alone in here wondering what's happening and I'm going to have litters of kittens. I love you, lunkhead.'

'And I love you, little one. I want you unshredded.'

'I'm a mean girl with a shoo . . . with a gun. You need me.'

She fired a look of utter determination at him. Unfolding her arms, she strode to the desk, where he had tucked away the two remaining 9mm Type 59s plus silencers and ammunition. She took out one of the pistols and fitted her small hand around its butt with a grim smile. It sent a little thrill of excitement all the way up her bare brown arm. 'If you absolutely refuse to let me come along, I'm going to give you absolute shit all day long.'

Forbes was aghast. 'But, Leila, Jesus, you know . . .'

'What's more,' she interrupted, 'when you get your usual attack of the hots before the action, you'll find that my *chocho*' – somewhere she had picked up a Spanish word for 'pussy' – 'will be strictly out of bounds.'

He managed a weak grin. He was defeated, and he knew it. He nodded at the pistol. 'Oil it. Then oil it again. Take it up to the forest at Los Nagueles and get in some practice.' His gaze swept longingly over her. 'And don't have any knickers on early this evening.'

The others spent the day apart, for the most part relaxing, preparing their minds for the imminent assault. They were to regroup at ten that evening, down on the beach half a kilometre from James Kennedy's house, where a *chiringuito* – a beach bar – stayed open until the early hours.

By eight-thirty they were each trying to contain their nervous tension in different ways.

The fair was still in full swing. Johnnie, having picked up a just short of tawdry bit of English holidaymaker skirt, was groping the girl and sipping whisky from a small hip-flask as they made trip after dizzying trip on a Ferris wheel as high as a twenty-storey apartment block. He was most careful with the whisky. His was going to be the most dangerous job later on; he was going to be more vulnerable than the others. The slightest error of judgement could cost him his life – and not simply at the hands of Sheikh Sulman's thugs.

Roldán, alone, was attacking one of the most expensive meals of his life in the French restaurant Silk's in Puerto Banús, taking his time about it, trying to blank his mind and concentrate solely on the food.

Tristram MacDowell was lustily making the two-backed beast with his $200 whore from the Marbella Club.

Freddie Fraser, who had days before discovered a little Spanish bar in the town where he could indulge his passion for the language-barrier-breaking game of chess, was reluctantly abandoning a match which had been going on for three hours. He had the task of being near James Kennedy's house before nine to make sure the sheikh showed up.

Keegan, who was trying to stop himself from craving to be elsewhere – salmon fishing in County Cork, for example, on the peaceful River Lee, or even mending someone's ancient toaster in Parsons Green, anything but sitting on this keg of dynamite, damn Forbes and his twenty grand to hell and back – was trying to murder both his opponent and the ball in the squash courts at Puente Romano.

And Forbes himself was riding a magnificent sexual high in the loving arms of his little lady; Leila, as keyed up as him with excitement, had obeyed orders and neglected to wear her knickers.

As the boss and his wife climbed the stairway to heaven, Freddie Fraser, walking from where a taxi had dropped him off, arrived at the final bend in the narrow lane which Sulman's convoy would be obliged to negotiate before arriving at James Kennedy's rambling old villa fifty metres further towards the beach. Hiding himself among some mature eucalyptus trees, he waited.

The three cars, Sheikh Sulman as usual at the wheel of the red Mercedes 280SL, rolled slowly down the lane at precisely nine o'clock, Freddie observing from deep shadow. As they approached the bend, a Harley-Davidson motor bike came speeding up behind them and overtook them, cutting sharply in front of the leading Merc 600 to roar around the bend.

Beyond a slightly raised eyebrow at the recklessness of the biker, Freddie took very little notice of him.

18

Her name was Blanca Nieve, Snow White in Spanish. She stood a solid sixteen and a half hands, was heavy-necked and broad of beam, and the fiery blood of the Andalusian horse pulsed in her veins. She weighed as much as the average fighting bull, around half a ton.

Overriding protests from Hammid Mullah – such mares could be hired by the hour, had been his argument – Forbes had bought her on Johnnie's recommendation several days before for 450,000 pesetas. They had taken a day trip to the home of some of the finest horses in Spain, Jerez de la Frontera, to pick her, and had had her driven in a horse box to Marbella to be liveried in a stable close to San Pedro.

Since then, apart from his tour of duty up in the pine tree, Johnnie had ridden the mare for three hours each day and one at night, both in the countryside and the arena. She was not the most wonderful horse in the world – they didn't come that cheap – but she was perfect for the job. No show mare, she was as reliable a hack and jumper of hedges and ditches as they came, instantly responsive to the lightest touch of the rein, the slightest body language of her rider or kiss of the heel in her muscular flanks.

Johnnie was a superb horseman, and good horseflesh thoroughly appreciates such a rider on its back. By D-day, beast and man were as thoroughly attuned as the insides of a wind-up watch.

At ten p.m. on Friday evening, Forbes, Leila and the rest of them with the exception of Johnnie were sitting around Pedro's *chiringuito* fully psyched up for the action ahead of them, willing time to pass and thus effectively slowing it down.

Johnnie came cantering along the edge of the moonlit sea towards the beach bar on the massive, startlingly white mare, a vision of manhood at its most macho. He was wearing tight black jeans tucked into a fine pair of riding boots, and a frilly white shirt. Hanging on his back from a string, rising and falling with the elegant motion of the horse, was a rigid, flat-topped riding hat. Surf was arcing up beneath the belly of the mare and spraying high behind her flying hooves.

Just before reaching the bar, Johnnie slowed the mare to a walk. Her nostrils flaring, and panting from the excitement of the gallop rather than the exertion, she brought her rider up the sloping sand. He slipped to the ground. Ignoring the others, Johnnie tied Blanca Nieve's reins to one of the wonky poles which closed off the bar's eating area, clomped across the wooden floor and ordered a sherry. Taking it back to his animal, he remounted and sat very tall in the saddle, sipping his drink and gazing out to sea while the horse performed the occasional little dance beneath him as she calmed down.

During this performance, there had not been a single eye in the bar which had not watched it. Leila's were fixed on Johnnie. God, she was thinking, you gorgeous bastard son of a bitch, aren't I tense enough without you parading your animal sexuality like fucking Don Juan himself? She could not help it, the man looked so unbelievably handsome atop his noble beast that he was arousing her despite what had been a growing aversion to him. Piss off, Johnnie, leave me in peace. Her scarlet-painted nails dug into Forbes's forearm.

Relief washed over her when, a quarter of an hour later, Johnnie finished his sherry, called for the waiter to take his glass and trotted off along the sand.

'Time to move,' said Forbes quietly. If he had noticed Leila's reaction to the horseman, he failed to mention it.

One by one they paid. Leila and Forbes walked off hand in hand down the beach, the others dispersed in slightly different directions. They regrouped several minutes later on the far side of a clump of eucalyptus trees from James Kennedy's villa. Apart from a smudge of moonlight seeping through the branches, it was comfortingly dark there. There was a little-used lane which petered out to nowhere. Just off this lane, parked among more trees were two hired black Range Rovers.

Without a word the little band of mercenaries hurried about their appointed tasks, checking their pistols, fixing the silencers and making sure the ammunition clips were fully loaded and slotted squarely into place. They hid three heavy-duty car batteries at ten-metre intervals behind trees on either side of the lane and wired searchlights into the branches above each of them. They attached the lights, switched off, to the batteries.

With the hour of eleven approaching, they pulled black hoods down over their faces and took up their positions.

A faint breeze rustled the leaves all around them. The nearby Mediterranean, invisible from there, but close, made a hypnotically rushing sound as it scudded long, lazy waves up on to the beach. A cicada, sounding like a whole swarm of insects all by itself, was chirruping away. The air was full of the sweet smell of night-blooming jasmine. A perfect night for romance.

Eleven-ten. The jarring groan of a not far distant, creaking hinge. The ancient iron gates of the Kennedy villa were being opened by a houseboy. Seconds later, the lane in front of the bend around which the gates lay hidden from the mercenaries became bathed in the glow of advancing headlights.

Forbes's keen eye roved up the lane in the direction of the highway. Where the fuck was Johnnie?

Everyone was trying to melt into the trunk of their grey-barked eucalyptus, silenced Chinese pistols clawed in sweaty, black cotton-gloved hands.

The big black Merc was followed by the red 280SL. They could see a little, white silk hat within. Then came the black-windowed Cadillac. The convoy was moving very slowly, as speed was inadvisable on this narrow, rutted country lane. The lead car was fifty metres away, and closing in.

Where the fuck *was* Johnnie?

Perfect timing. Galloping down the lane straight into the glare of the big Merc's headlights, his huge horse like some frightening phantom of the night, came Johnnie, his hat flying in his slipstream.

Mouths gaped, startled eyes grew wide inside the Merc at this sudden apparition, at this mad horseman galloping towards them in the moonlight.

There was something seriously wrong. The horse was swerving, bucking, rearing. It was terrified of the big headlights which were blinding it; except that it was not terrified at all – it was far too well trained for that. It was responding to the precision instructions of its rider.

The mare was almost upon them. The driver of the big Merc slammed on his brakes. The other cars stopped, no more than two metres between each of them, behind it.

Snorting and whinnying – but with excitement, not fear – the huge white horse brushed past the first car, its flanks bumping into the windows. Reaching the bonnet of the sheikh's little red Merc, it reared up high on its back legs, kicking its forelegs into the air and stomping in that attitude through three hundred and sixty degrees as the man in the silk hat cowed down and his whore screamed.

The trick now was to slap a rein sideways across the horse's neck and yank hard while thumping the animal solidly in its ribs with the heel of your boot on the same side as the tugging rein. Johnnie had performed it on two occasions when stunt-riding.

It worked perfectly. With a raucous whinny, the mare toppled over, crashing on to the bonnet of the red Merc, crumpling it into its engine. A hoof splintered the toughened glass window. Johnnie fell skilfully off his mount and rolled into the dust as Blanca Nieve crashed on to her side between the two cars.

All the doors of the escort cars swung open at once and the startled bodyguards spilled out into the lane.

They were suddenly, blindingly, bathed in white as the searchlights were switched on. One heavy made the mistake of reaching for his gun. Freddie, closest to him, shot him dead, the 9mm bullet tearing through his cheekbone just below his left eye.

'Hands high, *high*!' bellowed Forbes. Nine pairs of beefy arms reached for the stars. Then he dived for the crushed Merc. Screaming, Marian was erupting from it. He cracked a backhander around her face, splitting her cheek with his ring.

'Shut up!'

Silenced, blubbering, the girl fell to her knees beside the struggling horse. Grabbing the sheikh by the elbow, Forbes thrust his pistol into his nose and dragged him from his car. 'Go, go, go,'

he shouted as he heaved Sulman towards the
clump of trees behind which the Range Rovers
were parked.

Nobody noticed that the boot of the Cadillac
had opened wide enough for the nose of an
Ingram MACII machine-pistol to sneak out until
the gun began to spit death.

The boot opened wider. The gunman began to
rise to his knees from within, spraying bullets
into the glare. Johnnie was cut down, his chest
ripped open, lips twisting into a final, Cary
Grant rictus grin. The Irishman went a split
second later, his last, fading vision Cork City
and the River Lee as his heart exploded.

Forbes, Leila ahead of him, clinging to Sulman's
skinny arm, found the relative safety of the trees
as the heavies went for their guns. Tristram
MacDowell took four Arabs before he, too,
died, bullets from the Ingram stitching across
his forehead, cutting his brain in two.

Luis Roldán put an end to the carnage. Firing
his Type 59 pistol at the searchlights with his
left hand, he whipped out his throwing knife
with his right and sent it slicing through the
air with deadly accuracy; it buried itself to the
hilt through the right eye of the man in the boot
and the Ingram fell silent.

There were only three bodyguards left standing, one of them wounded. They dived for cover

into the Cadillac and slammed the bulletproof doors as Forbes, one hand keeping the sheikh's arm wrenched up hard behind his back, took careful aim and shot out a tyre of each of the Arabs' cars.

Bianca Nieve, none the worse, was fighting its wobbly-legged way to its feet. Next to it, Marian, in shock, swayed slack-mouthed on hands and knees. Her head, its long blonde hair trailing in the bloody dust, was bobbing around and up and down like that of a toy-dog mascot in the rear window of a moving car.

There was the sudden, throaty roar of a powerful engine. Through all the destruction, head down, leaning flat over its handlebars, sped a man on a Harley-Davidson. Forbes, fearing yet more aggression from this character, whoever he was, took aim at him but did not fire. The biker, followed by the bolting mare, her legs pounding, mane flying, and neighing in fright, accelerated away down the lane.

Freddie's left arm was gushing arterial blood. Trying to staunch the flow with his right hand, he struggled into the back seat of one of the Range Rovers. As Forbes shoved Sulman in after him, Fraser, heedless of his bleeding, grabbed the sheikh by a handful of collar and tie and dragged him up inside. Roldán ducked in behind Sulman, slamming the door. Leila scrambled up behind Forbes in front and he gunned the car away.

Engine screaming, the Range Rover slithered around in a wide arc, throwing up powdery dust and small stones. On the other side of the clump of eucalyptus trees the surviving Arabs were again leaving their Cadillac. None of them made any attempt to give chase.

Leila remained utterly cool. So much had gone fatally wrong, but they had their man. She followed her pre-attack instructions without being reminded. While Forbes changed plan, bumping them over a rutted field with no lights on, she stuck the needle of a hypodermic syringe into Sulman's arm and emptied sodium pentathol into it. The powerful barbiturate went straight to his nervous system and he passed out.

'Put the lights on?' she said. 'Don't get us killed, now.'

'Didn't you see the biker?' Forbes grunted. 'He could be one of them. Maybe he's lying in wait for us on the lane. If I show lights he might hit our tyres from there.'

'And risk puncturing his boss?'

Forbes cursed as the Range Rover plunged into an unseen dip in the field, reared up and crashed down, jolting them all off their seats. Almost any other type of vehicle would have rolled over with that sort of impact. Hands fighting the wheel, he regained control and slowed down.

'At some point I have to get us back on the lane. If that guy spots us and he happens to have a machine-pistol he won't miss the tyres.' Forbes panted the words, his adrenalin still seething.

Sulman was deeply unconscious, his head lolling and bouncing on Roldán's shoulder.

Freddie had ripped his shirt sleeve up to his shoulder. He was trying to hold a slippery, blood-drenched hand and thumb over a pressure point in an artery of his upper left arm, but he kept losing his grip with each lurch of the car. The next time this happened warm blood splashed forward on to Leila's shoulder.

'Christ!' she exclaimed. It was the first time she had noticed the seriousness of the wound, and the cockney had not complained. His arm, three inches up from the elbow, appeared to be half ripped away; there was blood everywhere. Tearing her thin chiffon scarf from her neck and taking a ballpoint pen from her bag, Leila leant over the seat. She twisted the chiffon until it formed a tight cord, wrapped it around the pressure point Freddie had been clinging to, knotted it, thrust the pen through the knot and began to turn it.

When they hit the lane there was no sign of the biker. Leila's makeshift tourniquet was by then working. The blood now only oozed, but her hands were soaked in it and a second gout had hit her full on the chin, to drip and trickle down her neck and the front of her thin blouse. She looked like the victim of a serious road accident.

Having thus far borne his pain and blood-letting without a murmur, Freddie now produced a weak grin. 'Keep your Dracula's daughter fangs away from me, there's a doll,' he said.

On arriving back at Casa Puck ten minutes later, they were faced with the problem of a beige-uniformed security guard hanging around outside smoking. Forbes turned off the engine and gave the house key to Leila. The inside of the Range Rover was awash with Fraser's blood; it was over everybody except Forbes. If the guard noticed the state they were in he was bound to react.

Jumping out of the car, Forbes hurried excitedly to the man, pointing up the narrow road. 'I saw something back there,' he said. 'Didn't look at all right.'

'*Qué*?' said the guard. Typical of his breed, he spoke not a word of English.

Forbes took him by the elbow and urged him up the slightly sloping road. 'Come quickly,' he said. '*Ven. Ven.*' As he coaxed the perplexed man away and then into an alley between two bungalows, Leila jumped down from the Range Rover to offer her bloody shoulder to Roldán, who pulled the drugged sheikh from inside. Between them they hauled him to the bungalow door, his patent-leather shoe points scraping along the asphalt, with Freddie lurching along like a drunk behind them. She let them in. No prying eye had noticed the bloody party.

The private ambulance from Ambulancias Costa del Sol was ordered for twelve forty-five, which gave them fifty minutes to clean themselves up and get ready. Forbes was going in the ambulance to Málaga Airport with Sulman. Leila and the other two were to take a taxi to the same destination.

The Range Rover, hired as it had been with a false passport, had to be dumped. While Roldán was taking care of this last little detail, Leila cleaned, disinfected and bandaged Freddie's nasty wound with items from the first-aid box, making a thoroughly good job of it as he fortified himself with liberal slugs of Forbes's Glenmorangie straight from the bottle.

The ambulance arrived exactly on time. Two attendants took great care in lifting the dangerously ill, pyjama-clad sheikh – now minus his little hat and the bearer of a genuine Kuwaiti passport in the prestigious name of the al-Sabah family but with Sulman's photo franked within

— on to their canvas stretcher and carrying him to the vehicle. As they turned out into the heavy Friday night traffic and the driver unnecessarily switched on his siren, a taxi for Leila, Freddie, Roldán and their luggage pulled up outside Casa Puck.

Hammid Mullah would take care of the final details in the morning. He would settle the Marbella Club bill, and there would be nothing to connect the evening's bloody happenings with respectable Mr and Mrs Stephen Forbes.

The final part of the operation went without a hitch. The ambulance was given special clearance to rush the illustrious sick Kuwaiti and his personal doctor out to the waiting Kuwaiti Air Force plane. No one thought to question why the doctor himself did not board the plane. Why should anyone care?

At three-fifteen, Forbes, Leila and the other two were boarding a Virgin Airways package-tour flight to Gatwick. At three thirty-five they were airborne.

As they sat in silence it was impossible for any of them to feel any elation at their success, or for Forbes and Leila to celebrate the imminent replenishment of their coffers with nearly half a million pounds when three admired and valued men were lying, barely cold, on slabs of pale-pink marble in Marbella mortuary, and a fourth corpse had been flown home for burial by arrangement with the man's widow the week before.

19

It was twelve-twenty on Tuesday morning and Forbes was thoroughly pissed off. He had slept the sleep of the exhausted all day Saturday and it had been understandable that nobody but a security man could be raised at the Kuwaiti Embassy on Sunday; but the fact that he could not get through to the ambassador on Monday was inexcusable. To add insult to injury, having finally obtained an appointment for ten-thirty this morning, here he still was, cooling his heels in that nightclubby reception room at the embassy waiting for his summons to Khalet Awadi's illustrious presence.

He recrossed his worsted-clad legs for the umpteenth time, taking great care to adjust the razor-sharp creases so that they would not be spoiled. He was immaculately and expensively dressed in a charcoal-grey, double-breasted, Chester Barrie suit, the softest of pink silk shirts with a semi-stiff white collar and a hand-knitted, deep-blue silk tie. On his feet were gleaming, black, completely plain shoes of the finest leather. Every inch the City banker, he would have been enjoying the change of persona after all the blood and guts down in Marbella had it not been for this jumped-up Arab arsehole screwing him around.

The British press had got hold of only scant details about Forbes's mission. It had not made a single front page. Reports had trickled through of some sort of a mini gang war down on the Costa del Sol involving some Englishmen and some Arabs, but neither names nor casualty figures had been released. Forbes supposed the Spanish authorities to be playing this one as quietly as they possibly could; blood-baths in holiday heaven at what was approaching peak season would not exactly be a boost for business. Nor did the newspapers mention anything about a kidnapping. They clearly had not got wind of it, and it was highly unlikely that Sheikh Sulman's closest associates would want to make a splash of it.

He got to his feet and wandered for perhaps the tenth time over to the french windows, which, in deference to an unusually hot June day, were open on to a balcony. He stepped outside. For a change, London was as warm as Marbella, but it did not smell particularly healthy. Below him, Queensgate was choked with traffic, its invisible fumes hanging heavy in the humid air. For a while he stood there on the balcony, contemplating the hustle and bustle, taking comfort in the fact that his lifestyle, perilous at times though it might be, did not involve him in the tedious routine that was the lot of a large proportion of the people scurrying about below him.

'Mr Forbes, sir?'

It was the poker-faced menial with the hooked nose. The ambassador would see him now. Snooty little bugger, thought Forbes as he followed the man along the gaudily lit, windowless passage. As they approached Awadi's office, Hammid Mullah walked smartly out of it, a bulging file clutched in his hand, a supercilious expression stretched thinly over his face.

'Good morning,' said the accountant briskly.

Already intensely aggravated by having been kept waiting for an excessive amount of time even by Arab standards, Forbes felt that the last person he wanted to bump into that morning was Mullah. Beyond an expressionless slithering of his eyes from the man's face to his fussy shoes and back up again as they passed one another, he ignored him.

'Two hours and seven minutes you've kept me waiting, Mr Awadi,' grumbled Forbes, checking his watch, as he lowered himself into the chair in front of the ambassador's desk. 'Way over the top, my friend.'

Awadi disregarded the complaint. Baldly, he said: 'You got the wrong man.'

A slug with a baseball bat to the back of the head might have had a lesser effect on Forbes than those five little words. He was as stunned as he had ever been in his life. The oily face before him, behind its tidy black beard, moustache and gold-rimmed spectacles, went out of focus as he stared, speechless, at it.

'He was a look-alike. A double by the name of Khalid Badria. He wasn't Sheikh Sulman at all.'

Forbes found his voice. 'Your people have let him con them. He's winding them up.' His words seemed to him to be coming from somewhere else – the Salvation Army doss-house round the corner, for instance, where all the drunks, drop-outs and nutters in general grudgingly accepted charity.

'There is not the slightest shadow of a doubt. Sulman is safe and sound in his villa in Marbella.'

His mind reeled back towards recovery. Sick to his stomach, Forbes knew that the man had to be telling the truth. Yet he said: 'You wouldn't be trying to wriggle out of the half a million, would you?'

Awadi sighed. He shook his head slowly, frowning at him, silently admonishing him.

'Yeah. I'm sorry,' muttered Forbes.

'I accept that this is a massive shock to you, Mr Forbes. I'll therefore ignore your insinuation.' Awadi fitted a cigarette into his holder and lit it. He shuffled some pieces of paper on his desk. 'A cock-up, I believe the English expression is, is it not?'

'Do me a favour? Don't shove my face in it?' Forbes just managed to bite the additional word 'arsehole' off the tip of his tongue.

'How did it happen?'

'Christ. When I've thought it through I'll let you know.'

The ambassador picked up a sheet of paper, scanned it, and read aloud from it. 'Ninety-one thousand, three hundred and seventy-four pounds,' he said. He looked up at Forbes. 'And fifty pence.'

'Which is?'

'The cost of your negative enterprise to us. Six times five thousand advance on manpower, thirty thousand. The purchase of a horse, two thousand two hun . . .'

'OK, OK. Jesus!'

'I am personally responsible for every penny expended through this embassy.'

'Kuwait has more crude under it than any-where in the world except Saudi. At seventeen dollars a barrel a hundred grand probably represents less than a split second's production.'

'A beautifully stated irrelevancy.'

'True.'

Forbes let his troubled eyes wander around the room as Awadi sucked silently on the carved-ivory business end of his cigarette-holder. The set of hunting prints, the vulgarly framed reproduction of Goya's *Naked Maja*, the even more ostentatiously framed portrait of the ruler of Kuwait behind the ambassador's head, all failed to register on his brain, which, struggling back into gear, was trying to work out where everything had gone wrong.

'Four men lost for nothing,' he muttered. 'Four first-class men.'

'And arms presumably continuing to pour into Iraq courtesy of Sheikh Yasser Sulman.'

Silence.

Awadi's eyes slid back to the statement of expenses. 'A horse, Mr Forbes? May I ask why on earth you found it necessary to buy a *horse*? We're hardly in the Middle Ages.'

Forbes told him at length. As he finished, Awadi was starting another cigarette. 'Ingenious,' the ambassador commented.

'It worked.'

'Up to a point. You lost four men and grabbed the wrong one.'

Forbes hardly needed to be reminded yet again. But he let it pass. 'They had a guy riding shotgun in the boot of the Cadillac with an opening device on the inside.' He sighed heavily. 'I never heard of that one. Christ, the man's better protected than Clinton.'

'Except for the fact that he wasn't even there.'

The celebrated Forbes hackles rose. He took a very deep breath, doing battle with his temper. 'I sincerely *would* leave the commentary alone now, if I were you, Ambassador,' he said, struggling to keep his voice under control. 'You see before you a very unhappy man. You see before you a man who can turn spiteful when he's unhappy. You've had the last word three times at least. I would hate our wonderful relationship to be threatened by a punch in the mouth.'

It was Awadi's turn to get angry. Tiny muscles twitched in his face. His thin nostrils flared. Carefully, glaring at it as if it had committed a mortal sin, he laid his smoking cigarette and holder across a silver ashtray. A vein bulged in his temple.

But the Kuwaiti was a highly experienced and skilful diplomat. Despite everything, he did not want to fall out with the dandily dressed, hired fighting machine sitting in front of him. He forced himself to calm down. 'Point taken,' he said.

'What's next?'

'I'm not sure. Apart from Saddam himself, Sulman remains the most important man on our wanted list.'

'Where does that leave me?'

'You came to us with immaculate references. The very best in your field. Naturally, I'm disappointed.'

'I *am* the best. I fucked up. It happened to Napoleon.'

'You believe there's still a chance you can get him out?'

'I miscalculated both his strength and his cunning.' Forbes adjusted his silk pocket handerchief, thinking hard. He flicked a speck of dust from his lapel. 'Nevertheless the fact remains that I'm a trained soldier with access to as many top-flight mercenaries as I need and he's a businessman surrounded by a bunch of semi-thick thugs. Of course I can get him out.'

'Presumably not employing the same approach again?'

'Presumably.' Forbes got to his feet. 'This morning's news has smacked me way below the belt. I'm still in shock. I have to sort my head out. Give me twenty-four hours, we'll meet here again, OK? I need to work out what happened, why it happened.' He buttoned his jacket. 'I'll bring you a fresh proposition first thing tomorrow.'

'Which is going to cost us a whole lot more money?'

'Without doubt, my friend.'

Awadi's eyes roved over the expenses sheet once again. He shrugged, but he did not look happy. 'Just as long as you come up with the goods this time.'

'I will.'

'I'll want you to outline a sensible plan. It'll need my approval.'

'OK. I told you, tomorrow.'

The ambassador stood. 'But I wouldn't expect any increase in my personal fee if I were you.'

'I won't ask. We already have a deal.'

'Exactly.'

'Do me one big favour?' Forbes asked, his big mitt engulfing Awadi's beringed claw in a parting handshake. 'Don't keep me waiting again in the morning, there's a good chap. Please?'

'The fucking man on the fucking motor bike,' Forbes growled at Leila, seconds after dropping the devastating news.

'There you go again.'

'You'd better believe it.' Filled with self-contempt bordering on loathing, he fixed himself a formidable slug of Glenmorangie. 'What an idiot. What a bloody short-sighted, moronic clown I am.'

'Whoa there. Tell me about the, um, effing man on the effing motor bike?' Leila was trying to stay light-hearted. Despite the disappointment raging within her, she was not about to let it show if she could avoid it when her man was so patently low.

They were back in a suite at the Savoy where they had been planning, apart from how to spend some of it, ways and means of safely investing the bulk of the half a million pounds Forbes was now not about to pick up. He had his doubts that the Kuwaitis were even going to pick up the tab for the Savoy, under the circumstances.

'I noticed the biker two or three times when I was watching Sulman's place. He appeared from around the side of it on what looked like a Harley. Stupid bastard that I was, I didn't take much notice. I should have checked it out, of course, I should have checked out every tiny detail.' He swallowed his whisky like water. 'I'd have been dead by now in Central America or the Congo. I'm slipping.' He turned irritated eyes on her. 'Christ, am I getting senile, or what?'

Comfort him, she told herself. 'You may be

senile but you're a better man in the sack than someone half your age.'

He managed a weak grin. 'How would you know?'

'What about the man on the bike?'

'Apart from my sightings, Freddie mentioned a biker in his report of the sheikh's arrival at James Kennedy's. A nutter cut them up, he said. Again, I took no notice. Finally there was the guy who came roaring through the battlefield. Remember I thought he might be another of them? Then he vanished?'

The light dawned. 'One and the same?' said Leila slowly, eyes wide. 'Sulman.'

'Slippery little son of a bitch. Of course it was. The death-dealer himself.'

Leila prised Forbes's glass from his fingers and took a pull at the Scotch. Not having realized it was undiluted malt, she spluttered out her next words. 'Well, lover, you've sure gotta hand it to him.'

'I guess.' He took the glass back, emptied it down his throat, poured another shot and two fingers for Leila, putting her glass into her hand. He chinked his tumbler against hers.

A spark of excitement was rekindling in Forbes's capricious belly. Sheikh Sulman was a worthy opponent. In any case, he had nothing personally against arms dealers – they were an essential part of his world. 'Here's to him,' he said. 'And to his eventual downfall at the hands of Squire Forbes.'

Leila pulled a wry little smile. 'And here's — for the second time — to our half a million smackers.'

He decided not to make an issue out of it. Keeping someone waiting eleven minutes was positively seeing them early by Arab standards. Awadi failed to apologize. He waved a careless hand at the chair in front of his desk and as Forbes sank into it he asked: 'Did you come to any conclusions?'

Forbes told him about the motor-bike ruse. How there had to be another exit somewhere, through the dog run perhaps.

'Then why did they shoot at you?' asked the ambassador. 'I mean, since they knew it wasn't Sulman at the wheel of his car but Khalid Badria?'

'We took one of them out first. In any case, they were his bodyguards. They'd have to defend the man, wouldn't they, otherwise any potential kidnapper would tumble it wasn't him.'

'Tumble?'

'Realize.'

'Oh.'

Awadi removed his glasses to clean them,

studying the lenses closely as he did so. Suddenly his curly-lashed eyes appeared smaller. He adjusted the glasses carefully on his nose and studied Forbes through them, steepling his fingers together and flattening the steeple under his chin. 'Any fresh ideas on the subject?'

'My brain's been working on nothing else.'

'Let me ask you something. Are you hungry, Mr Forbes?'

Forbes knew what he was driving at. Hunger breeds desperation. Desperate men will go for the jugular with an enhanced sense of cunning; clever, desperate men, that was. 'I'm hungry,' he said.

'Take me through it.'

Forbes told him, step by step, what he had worked out with a little help from Leila: a preliminary course of action followed by Plan A, then a contingency Plan B.

'I'm amazed. Your mind is most extraordinarily fertile,' said Awadi when Forbes fell silent.

'I eat Wheaties for breakfast.'

'Quite.' The ambassador appeared slightly bemused.

'Well?'

'I was wondering when you came in why you hadn't shaved this morning. Now I understand.'

Forbes fingered his twenty-four-hour growth of beard. He was not happy about it – it was pushing through more grey than brown. 'It occurred to me I'd better get started on it right away. It'll take a few days to fill out a bit.'

'You therefore anticipated you'd get the go-ahead from me?'

'Something of the sort.'

'Mmm. Assuming you manage to inveigle yourself into the position in Marbella which you have outlined to me, and I have a hunch you will, it would be most satisfactory if Plan A were to succeed.'

'Cheaper, you mean?'

'That as well, but it's hardly the number one priority.'

'I'm not entirely convinced Plan A's going to come off. It's worth a stab at, that's all.'

'I agree.' The ambassador got up and walked around his desk to perch himself on its corner and stare down at Forbes. 'Let us get some rough idea of costs?'

'A luxury villa for a month or two. I already put in a call to a Marbella estate agent. It's coming into high season. Fifteen thousand dollars a month is about the going rate.'

Awadi stretched for a pen and a notepad and jotted down the figure. 'That would include staff, electricity and so forth?'

Forbes nodded. 'And dog food.'

Flippancies such as that irritated the Kuwaiti

but he managed to ignore it. 'You won't know how big a team you will need until you've properly settled in and achieved the, ah, *status* you'll be looking for. But presumably there'll be less men for Plan A than B?'

'And weapons, yes. I'll probably need to build my team back to six for A, at least to a squad for B. And with rather more impressive fire-power than Chinese pop-pops.'

'Let's examine the maximum expense. A squad is how many?'

'A dozen. But I might need as many as twenty.'

'At our original figure? Twenty thousand pounds each?'

'Can do.' Forbes's mouth was dry. 'Do you have such a thing as a beer?'

'Naturally. This isn't the Saudi Embassy.' He pressed a button on his desk.

'Don't believe they don't have booze tucked away even there.'

Hook-nose came in and was dispatched for a lager and a Coca-Cola. While he was fetching them, Awadi shot Forbes a question about Leila.

'. . . so you see, she's just perfect for the part,' Forbes was saying as the drinks arrived and the menial departed. He took a swig from the glass of Skol. It was deliciously cool, welcome.

The day was hotter and more humid than the previous one and his scratchy growth of beard seemed to make the heat even worse. 'In a sense Leila's already got her face in Act One.'

'She has?'

As Forbes steadily downed the lager while the ice cubes began to melt in Awadi's untouched Coca-Cola, Forbes told the Arab about his and Leila's chance encounter with Lord and Lady Sandhurst in the Marbella Club bar.

'A good beginning,' commented the ambassador.

'I like it, yeah.'

'So. Let us say twenty men times twenty thousand.' Awadi made a note on his pad. 'Four hundred thousand pounds. Minus ten. Three hundred and ninety thousand.'

'What minus ten?'

'You're using your two survivors?'

'They'll be with me, sure.' Freddie Fraser never turned a job down and Luis Roldán was eager for bread.

'They've already been paid their signing-on fee.'

Forbes's sudden look of amazement turned into an angry glare. 'Who are you anyway – Mullah in disguise? Jesus, this is a fresh operation, man.'

Awadi sighed. 'All right, all right. Don't blow up in my face. It's a fresh operation.'

'OK, now we understand each other.' Forbes drained the last of his beer. 'If Plan A goes all right we won't need more than a couple more pistols to replace those we lost. But if it's the contingency plan, that's a whole new ball game. I very much doubt that your Madrid embassy will be able to supply what I'm going to need.'

'Which is?'

When Forbes had finished reeling off a small list of weaponry only used normally in full-scale war, the ambassador was blanching. 'I see what you mean. Where will you get them?'

'Maybe I'll try Sulman?'

'Please, Mr Forbes. That was not in the least funny.'

'Sorry. I can get them. I have the contacts. But they're not going to come cheap. Illegal arms, expensive in the first place, smuggled into a country which is engaged in almost open warfare with the ETA terrorists. Going to cost you an arm and a leg.'

The ambassadorial pen was poised. 'How much?'

'Look, why don't you stop scribbling things down? I'll give you a couple of round figures. If you're lucky and we get away with Plan A it'll cost you something short of a million quid. Plan

B, maybe as much as two million. Either way, it's peanuts, my friend.'

Awadi mouthed an unhappy smile. He finally took a pull at his Coca-Cola. 'Peanuts,' he repeated weakly.

20

The shabby doorway of number 23C Angel Place, off Finsbury Circus, was as disenchanting as the smooth, salesman's voice on the telephone had been inspiring earlier that morning. A depressing shade of brown, the door needed a fresh coat of paint and it made a sound like an asthmatic's wheeze as Forbes opened it. A small, tarnished chrome plaque by its side bore the words 'John Brittan Publishing Company' and below them 'Triumph Books'.

Sitting in muddled gloom in a small reception area within was a fattish young lady who was busy tweezering an eyebrow as Forbes and Leila approached her untidy desk. They had picked the company from one of those advertising in the *Daily Telegraph*'s Arts & Books section – a 'vanity publishing' outfit whose advertisement asked aspiring authors if their work truly deserved to be published.

Tucked under her arm, Leila was carrying in a cardboard file the ageing, dog-eared manuscript of Forbes's thriller. There was just one crisp new page, the title page; it had originally been called *The Weight of Justice*, but now it was *The Suicide Man*.

Forbes was wearing four days' growth of beard. He had had Leila tint out the grey, partially because he considered the beard and moustache were putting years on him, more essentially because the greyish-brown growth was as yet too sparse to photograph well.

Philip Jolly, speciality publisher, was a pleasant enough man holding fort in an office whose walls were liberally sprinkled with framed book covers which, on inspection, would not have conjured up memories of a single author who had made any impact on the world.

'Delighted to meet you,' said Jolly in a classiess voice as Forbes and Leila parked themselves before his desk. 'So that's the cherished work, is it?' he added, nodding at the torn green file which Leila was dumping on his desk.

'Not so much cherished as perished,' grunted Forbes.

'It's a tough world out there, Mr Scott.' Jolly reached for the file. 'Because you've been rejected several times doesn't mean the novel's a bad one. It may even be best-seller material. Look at *The Day of the Jackal* – it was chucked out four times.' This was his standard spiel.

'We want it in print as fast as possible,' Leila told him.

Slipping the manuscript from its file, Jolly began thumbing through its tired pages. 'I'll first have to have it read.'

'It doesn't matter about that,' said Forbes.

The remark induced a sharp look and an admonishing frown. 'With respect, we don't publish just anything. We have our reputation. In any case, we won't get sufficient distribution to show a profit with just any pile of . . .' – he stopped the word 'junk' from spilling from his lips – 'not that I anticipate this to be anything but first-class.'

'Bull,' said Leila, enjoying herself.

'I beg your pardon, young lady?'

Forbes grinned. 'I believe my wife means how much.'

'That's all very well. We . . .'

'I want it published – immediately. I want a clean, attractive job as fast as possible.'

'But, Mr Scott . . .'

'How *much*, Mr Jolly?'

The publisher rifled through all the pages quickly; there were three hundred and fifty-three of them in double-spaced quarto. He appeared confused, his greyish eyes darting over the final page without actually reading. Used to dealing with people who were more often than not slightly retiring, fairly naïve hopefuls whom he tried to pursuade that he was the man to make their dreams come true, suddenly he found himself confronted with a couple who were anything but the usual type. He glanced at the clean front page.

'We'll have to find a better title for it.'

'It's the title, Mr Jolly,' said Forbes.

'But . . .'

'It's the *title*. I won't have it changed.'

'Very well.' Huffy. 'It'll need editing – and don't take offence over that, even Frederick Forsyth is edited,' said Jolly, laying the manuscript flat before him and tapping it with one finger.

'Forget it. It's edited.'

'But, Mr Scott . . .'

'It's edited.'

The man shook his head, beaten. 'Then there's the cover. We'll have one or two alternative designs drawn up for you to choose from. We'll . . .'

Leila thrust a hand-designed, coloured book jacket before him. She had produced it herself and it compared favourably with most on the market.

'Cover,' said Leila. 'And, here.' She gave him a photograph of Forbes with his dyed beard, and a negative. It had been taken that morning and developed by a one-hour-service shop. 'Photo. The entire back of the jacket, please.' She smiled. 'Don't you think Stephen looks distinguished?'

'Well, yes, um . . .'

'Fifty copies, make them weighty, one week maximum,' said Forbes.

'Only fifty?'

Leila fluttered her eyelashes at him. 'We have a launch party.'

'A what? How on earth can you have a launch party? Who's going to distribute, for God's sake? Don't you realize you should have your distribution properly in place before any party?'

'Can you do it or not?' asked Forbes, rising. He held out his hand. 'There are plenty of you people around.'

Philip Jolly was beginning to sniff money. 'It's going to be full of mistakes,' he warned.

'Just get it done the best you can. I'll take it warts and all.'

'And it's going to be pricey. It'll need to be set up in parallel sections or it will never be ready in time.' He fell silent, waiting for a reaction.

Forbes said nothing. He simply stared.

'And I'm afraid it makes no difference that you only want fifty copies. You'll have to pay for a minimum print run.

'Well?'

'Ten thousand pounds,' Jolly said abruptly, flinching within at his audacity.

From his inside jacket pocket, Forbes fished some bundles of £50 notes. As the publisher tried to keep his eyes from bulging, he tossed two of the bundles on his desk. 'Two grand,' he said. 'The rest on delivery. In exactly one week from now or you know what you can do with the books. As good a job as you can produce, OK?'

'Yes, well. Well, naturally, Mr Scott, Mrs ...' Jolly gathered up the money, wondering about the extraordinarily favourable position his stars must be in on this fine day. He could do the job for half and still show a profit.

'Oh, and here's the blurb about the author,' said Leila, getting to her feet as she handed a typed sheet of quarto to the man. 'Make sure it goes in doubly proofread, please – exactly as it's written.' It was a glowing profile of the academic Stephen Scott, cobbled together by the two of them amid a certain amount of hilarity the night before.

'Yes, yes, of course,' said the shaken publisher as they made to leave.

'Ta-ra for now,' Leila gaily called over her shoulder.

Outside, on the dusty pavement. Leila grabbed Forbes's arm and tucked herself into his side, rubbing her cheek on the lapel of his jacket, smiling up at him. 'What do you know, you're gonna be famous, lover,' she trilled.

'Or dead,' said Forbes.

21

The bloody people were being more fussy than buyers, thought Francine as she drove Forbes and Leila away from the third house they had rejected. It was the beginning of July, and there weren't many places left to rent. What the hell did they expect for a month or two?

She chuckled at a remark which Forbes, sitting beside her, had passed about a stray ginger cat. He said it looked like Lady Thatcher on the prowl. She cast a sideways glance at him. Well, not really *bloody*, she decided. Just difficult. And the blonde – Leila had dyed her hair – was gorgeous.

Were it simply a question of a holiday, Forbes would have been content with any of the three villas this charming, attractive English lady had shown them. They had each been in the super-luxury class, with pools and servants, ideal to laze away a summer within but short of perfect for his purpose. The last one, for instance, a beautiful, sprawling, rustic-style house with acres of wooden beams, had a driveway which was overlooked by two other homes. Naturally he had not been able to tell Francine that that was his only reason for rejecting it. She would have thought he was slightly crazy since the half acre of front garden was completely secluded and one hardly spent one's time on the drive.

Near to the Marbella Club, the estate agent pulled off the highway on the mountain side of the road. She was perplexed. If they didn't like the last three, she thought, they were unlikely to go for this one. But since they were being impossible anyway, one never knew.

'Exclusive little area,' she told them as she drove along a bumpy access road, then took a right turn past the imposing entrance to a villa on their left and a thick hedge. They followed the lane through a right-angled left turn and on past the hedge on one side and huge, yellowy-brown canes overhanging the other. The lane was narrow and badly kept, here and there disintegrating, and occasionally the leaves of the canes brushed the side of the car.

'Only five houses,' Francine went on, 'and just the one way in and out of here, so it's very private. No tourists wandering around.'

Forbes studied the surroundings with keen

interest as they turned left again and passed a crooked, worn, arrow-shaped sign with
'Ramptona' painted on it.

'Ramptona?' asked Leila. 'Like the nuthouse
with an "a"?'

'I'm afraid so.' Francine smiled. 'The owners
are possessed of a slightly bizarre sense of
humour. British aristocracy, you understand.'
She turned right between two very high, thick
hedges to ascend a steepish, ungated drive.

'Not Lord and Lady Sandhurst's house by
any chance?' asked Forbes, knowing full well
it was not.

'No, Stephen' – Francine was very quick at
getting on first-name terms with her clients, her
bubbly personality smoothing the intimacy – 'the
Foleys, actually. They've gone off to America for
the summer.'

'I see.' The name meant nothing to him. But
he liked what he was seeing. The garden was
steep and lovely with lots of flowers and bushes
and some twisted olive trees and a pool up in a
secluded corner. The drive opened wide at the
rear of the house, where the entrance was fronted
by a set of stone steps.

As Francine parked at the bottom of the steps,
a German shepherd in front of a kennel set up
a racket, barking and dancing about on the end
of a chain. She left the car and went up to pet

it. 'There, there, Pancho, it's all right, boy,' she said. The dog immediately calmed down, its bark changing to an excited whimper.

'Even on good terms with the dogs, eh?' said Forbes as he walked up the flight of steps, looking around. This, he thought, was it. A perfectly secluded area, and the car park was backed by a hedge three or four metres high, totally private.

Francine went past him, her white, high-heeled shoes clicking on the stone. She rang a bell by the side of a pair of ancient wooden doors. 'Not all of the dogs, darling,' she said. 'But these people are personal friends of mine, you see. I visit here a lot when they're in residence. Play bridge and so forth.'

A dumpy little maid let them into an imposing entrance hall the height of the house, with a marble floor and a marble staircase leading to a narrow mezzanine. There was a huge oil painting of a rather enigmatic-looking gentleman in ceremonial robes adorning one wall. Forbes read aloud from the inscription beneath it. 'Henry Thomas, 4th Lord Foley,' he said.

Francine produced her infectious little chuckle. 'One of the illustrious ancestors.' As she took them through into a spacious, bright and sunny drawing-room she was thinking, God, they're not going to like this one, either. She's young

217

and a bit of a swinger – it'll be a little too on the starchy side for her.

Forbes strolled through the room to where a panoramic sliding window gave on to a wide terrace with gardens dropping away from it. There was a beautiful view all the way down to the Mediterranean, something less than a kilometre away. The landscape was almost completely filled with trees and hedges, with just the odd corner of a building intruding here and there.

'Rather a *nice* house,' opined Francine. 'Very British in its way, I suppose, but personally I adore it. It's . . .'

'We'll take it,' said Forbes.

She blinked at him, remaining otherwise expressionless. 'But don't you even want to . . .?' She was about to say 'see the bedrooms' but Forbes interrupted her.

'How much?'

Francine met them again at Ramptona later that afternoon with a contract prepared for one month's rental and an option after three weeks to stay on for a second month. Forbes and Leila arrived from their hotel – not the Marbella Club this time, because he was someone else; he was Stephen Scott – in a taxi heaped with luggage. Francine showed up half an hour later.

'It's wonderfully peaceful here,' said Forbes

as he signed the contract in the name of Scott. 'Suits my purpose admirably.'

'Purpose?' echoed Francine.

'I'm not simply a lotus-eater,' he told her, amusing himself with the irony. 'I'm a novelist. I'll be working on a thriller.'

'How very interesting. Should I have heard of you? Come to think of it the name Stephen Scott does ring some sort of a bell.'

'Does it? I'm amazed.'

He got up from where they had been sitting on a sofa beneath a large painting of Rome in front of the Vatican three centuries ago, which might have been a Canaletto but was not – it was unsigned and unattributed – and went out into the hall to rip open the lid of one of two ponderous cartons of books they had brought with them.

Philip Jolly had overseen a commendable job. Eager to get his needy hands on the other eight thousand pounds in cash, worried that his strange client might not pay up, he had personally overseen the work to the extent of proofreading it twice himself. In point of fact he had actually enjoyed the story. Like its author's life it was pacey, and it was not at all badly written: it deserved a better fate than fifty copies.

'You've been very kind,' said Forbes as he

handed Francine a copy of *The Suicide Man*. 'Here. To say thank you.'

'Well, how super.' She turned the book over, glancing at the photo on the rear of the dust-jacket. 'Will you sign it for me?'

He did so with a flourish, beginning to enjoy his new identity.

As Francine was about to leave, Forbes had an afterthought. 'You must know a lot of people down here?' he asked her in the hall.

'Just about everybody, actually.' Her smile cracked a dimple.

'We don't know anybody apart from Lord and Lady Sandhurst – and you, of course. We'd like to have a bit of a social life while we're here. I wonder if you'd do something for me?'

'Arrange a party?'

'Just a small one. Thirty, forty people. Anybody you think we might get along with. I'll pay you, naturally.'

The dimple dented prettily again. 'Why not? It'll be a pleasure, Stephen.' She glanced at the book in her hand. 'No charge.'

'Leave the Sandhursts to me. I'll ring them.'

'Don't bother,' she said. 'They've popped over to Morocco for a week. I doubt if they'll come back from Marrakesh for a party, even for a famous author.'

As Francine's little car buzzed away down the

drive, Leila appeared at the top of the stairs. Looking up at her, Forbes was filled with tense excitement. Stage one was completed, stage two successfully under way. Leila began to walk down. She had on a miniskirt which from his point of view was most revealing. He started up the stairs, his eyes fixed on the white-cotton crotch of her knickers.

'About turn, sweetheart,' he said, the words rolling off his tongue.

'We still have to try out the matrimonial bed.'

The Scotts' little party, from the point of view of a couple trying to ease themselves into Marbella society, went off well. It did not open every door to them, but it oiled the hinges. It took place five nights after their moving in to Ramptona. Francine had been most careful and diplomatic with the guest list. She had not attempted to invite any of the kings and queens of the jet set; that would have been an enormous social gaffe, unhealthy for her reputation – there's this new couple in town, he's an author, simply would not do. No, the author would be so lucky if *they* invited *him*. All the same, she had managed to get together a bunch of the courtiers.

Forbes was not disappointed that there were no pals of Sheikh Sulman, no Baroness von

Pantz or Don Jaime de Mora or James Kennedy or Raymond Nakachian; he had not expected Francine to perform miracles. But there were Jaguars and Mercedes and BMWs parked on the drive, and there was a Rolls.

Forbes had discovered an upright piano in the semi-basement where the servants' quarters were. His lordship was a wonderfully accomplished pianist; there was also a Steinway grand but this was locked up in the music room, where the Foleys had stored their more valuable bits and pieces in case of a rental. Forbes had had the upright brought up on to the patio and employed a pianist from a nightclub in Puerto Banús. The do consisted of a cold buffet from a local delicatessen, served by two waitresses, and there was a proficient barman.

Leila, wearing a shimmering, multicoloured evening dress hand-sewn with thousands of sequins – curiously enough from Sarah Percival, who was a personal friend of the Foleys who had once given a fashion show around the pool of this very house – acted the perfect social butterfly, flitting from person to person, gaily chatting, while Forbes found himself repeatedly discoursing wisely on the art of being an author.

While Leila's objective was consocation, Forbes's was information. As he got into conversation with somebody new he would adopt one or other variation on the same theme. The author bit was most useful, though he had not made the show of spreading copies of the novel around as if this were a launch party; that would have been vulgar. He merely had one copy lying on a coffee table. But there was hardly anybody who upon first meeting him did not bring up the subject of his writing.

In most cases the conversation would follow similar lines. The person was delighted to meet Forbes, it made a change to have a bit of culture on the coast; or, most people here are such bores, or, I once met Harold Robbins, and so on. Were the Scotts planning on staying long? Was he working on a new book? Well-meant interrogation droned on until the subject grew thin, then it was Forbes's turn. There seem to be so many interesting people on the coast, he would remark – celebrities, titles, the super-wealthy, such a good place to inject new life into the jaded brain of an author. A bit more similar small talk, then, casually: 'I've heard there's this mega-rich Arab, an arms dealer or something of the sort, a sheikh who runs around with cars full of bodyguards?'

It seemed that none of the party guests enjoyed the status to have merited an invitation to Yasser Sulman's table. Some had never heard of him, many were vague. But here and there familiar names popped up – you'll have to speak to Terry or James about him, old boy – as if he didn't know – and twice a name arose which caused his ears to prick up.

The second time this occurred, Forbes was chatting with an amiable Dutchman, Dick Gobel, who had several times sailed the Atlantic single-handed in a small boat, and who had been recounting his experiences to Forbes because he understood that Stephen Scott had included a long passage about fighting a heavy sea in *The Suicide Man*.

'Oh, yeah,' said Gobel, when Forbes got around to the real subject of interest to him, 'that guy. I thought he was some sort of lunatic, you know? Paranoid about being bumped off, going everywhere surrounded by bodyguards. He must be totally nuts, I thought. Then there was some sort of shoot-out with his bodyguards, down near James Kennedy's place a couple of weeks ago.'

'Tell me about it,' said Forbes.

'Not a lot to tell. There were bodies, for sure, but it was hushed up. Say, you know who you should ask about the guy? Lord and Lady Sandhurst. They're apparently bosom pals of his. They've been spending half their lives in his house lately. They actually went to Morocco to take a rest from it, she told me so herself.

Apparently he was beginning to overwhelm them. Do you know them? I can give you an introduction if you like.'

'Thanks. I know them, yeah,' said Forbes distractedly. He had of course observed the sheikh's convoy park on the Sandhursts' drive from the air, and he had seen them visit him. But he had no idea they were so close. The Sandhursts, then.

Did she have any idea when Charles and Sophronia were due back? Forbes asked Francine a little later. She did – in just two days. They had taken the opportunity to go off to visit their relatives in Seville, and Francine had offered to slip a bit of fresh food in their fridge for their return.

'It's that Scott fellow,' Sophronia Sandhurst hissed to her husband, her knobbly, glittering hand over the mouthpiece of the telephone to which her ear was glued. She unclasped the hand. 'Yes, but of course we remember you,' she trilled. 'You what?'

Seconds later she said: 'Just a minute, I'll check,' blocking the mouthpiece again. 'He's rented the Foleys' house and he wants us to come to dinner. He's going to give us a signed copy of his book.'

'Book? What book?' Sandhurst asked through

a mouthful of the fresh smoked salmon which Francine had put in the fridge. He was getting muddled on Stolichnaya and tonic water.

'Yes, that will be lovely. Tomorrow at nine. We'll look forward to it. What? Yes, of course we know the house, Mister, um, Stephen. We'll be there.'

'Book? What book?' repeated Sandhurst when she hung up.

She sighed. 'He's a novelist. We met in the club bar, oh, it must be almost a month ago. What's happening to your memory, Charles? God.'

'You can't expect me to remember every blasted . . .' his eye sharpened. 'Had a cute little floozy with him, wasn't it? Sexy little piece?'

Lady Sandhurst sighed again. 'Yes, dear. His wife.'

The Sandhursts showed up the following evening twenty minutes late, considered reasonable timing on the coast, where the only real visiting sin was to be early – that was worse than forgetting to fasten your flies. Forbes himself, feeling that it was somehow friendlier than leaving it to the maid, opened the front door to receive them. Sandhurst had parked his vintage Bentley precisely across the bottom of the steps, thus making it a little awkward for any other guests to negotiate their way into the house.

But there were no other visitors. Forbes and

Leila had planned to have this couple entirely to themselves. Cultivation was the order of the evening; cultivation, buttering up, ego-brushing, call it what you will, Mr and Mrs Stephen Forbes were intent on charming the pants off Lord and Lady Sandhurst on this balmy summer evening, they were going to love them to death, to get themselves loved passionately in return.

It was part of a short-term plan, its fruition desired as soon as possible, to persuade these pillars of the British aristocracy to wangle the Scotts an invitation into the lion's den, into the lair of Sheikh Sulman.

'You're both somehow different, aren't you?' observed Sophronia as Forbes's beard tickled her while he kissed both her cheeks and she noticed Leila's change of hair colour.

'We enjoy a bit of variety. You're different, too. You look somehow younger than I remember you,' said Forbes.

As Leila was fixing them drinks, Sophronia said: 'I say, you certainly seem to have made a splash here, Stephen.'

'I'm not sure what you mean.'

'Just about everyone's talking about you, dear boy. The rising star on the coast, so it seems.'

Leila handed her a large glass of cold white Rioja, and a vodka tonic, heavy on the vodka

– he had remembered to get in a bottle of Stolichnaya – to her husband.

'Are they?' he said innocently. 'The damned book, I suppose.' He took a sip of his whisky. 'Francine's fault,' he lied. 'I asked her to keep quiet about it.'

'Why, is it porn?' asked Sandhurst.

Leila's little hand smacked the back of his in mock admonishment. 'Certainly not,' she laughed. 'It's a good old-fashioned thriller.'

'Anyway, we didn't invite you here to be bored with me,' put in Forbes. 'I'll give you your copy, then we'll shut up about it, shall we?'

He had signed it and written, 'To Lord and Lady Sandhurst, in memory of our first happy meeting and in hopes of a lasting friendship' above the signature.

'God, what a smarmy bullshitter you are,' Leila had remarked when she had watched him do it earlier, and he had laughed at her, saying: 'That's me, kiddo. Top of the class.'

'I understand you two are on friendly terms with some sheikh or other,' Forbes said casually, halfway through dinner.

'With two, as a matter of fact,' said Sophronia.

'Oh. This one I heard has lots of body-guards?'

'They both do. One's called Karechi and the other's Sulman.'

'Which one is the arms dealer?' Forbes asked innocently.

'Sulman, though he denies it.'

'I think that's the name I heard.'

'Y,' said Sandhurst.

'Why what?'

'No. Y. We call him Y. His name's Yasser, do you see? And he's an enigmatic little bugger, so we call him Y.'

Sophronia washed down a mouthful of roast lamb – which Leila had helped the maid to prepare – with the excellent white wine, a Marqués de Cáceres '64, the best Forbes had been able to find. 'He's been drugging my tea,' she said.

'I beg your pardon?' asked Forbes.

'I swear he's been putting something in my tea. He's been trying to hypnotize me, to get into my brain.'

'As long as that's the only place, old gel,' guffawed Sandhurst. He took a long pull at his drink. Vodka with everything, including lunch and dinner, that was his lordship. He addressed the table. 'Sophie's going a bit dotty lately. Got this obsession that Y's drugging her.'

'Well, he is.' Sophronia gave Forbes a confiding look. 'God knows why, but he's been trying to take us over. Through me. That last week before we went off to Morocco he insisted we dine with him every day. We spent more time in his house than in ours.'

'Cultivating the aristocracy,' observed Forbes with an ingratiating, aristocracy-cultivating smile.

'People do,' said Sandhurst. 'Lord knows why. You'd think we were royalty or something.'

'I heard about a shoot-out involving an Arab and his security men a short while ago. Wouldn't have been him by any chance?'

God, Leila was thinking, you should play Shakespeare, lover. What a ham!

'It was him, yes. He was leaving James Kennedy's house. James told me it sounded like bonfire night for a while. But Y never mentioned it,' said Sophronia.

Not our Chinese shooters making the racket, thought Forbes. They had silencers. It was that fucking murderous machine-pistol in the boot.

'Bodies all over the show, apparently,' Charles told them through the rim of his glass. 'Hushed up, though. Made the news and that was that. Rum sort of a business.' He frowned fiercely at his wife. 'If you ask me, we should stay well clear of the feller.'

'But nobody *is* asking you, my pet.'

Britannic conviviality – with the aid of the demon drink – ruled the waves. Having no wish to appear over-interested in it, Forbes had switched from the subject of the sheikh. To his delight, over coffee and liqueurs, Sophronia, immensely happy with her new-found friends, said: 'Y's coming to lunch with us on Thursday. Why don't you two join us?'

'I don't know if that's . . .' Sandhurst began.

Forbes cut in. 'That would be wonderful, Sophronia. I think we would enjoy meeting the man, wouldn't we, Leila?'

Later, as he let the Bentley take them home, the tanked-up Lord Sandhurst finished his earlier attempt at a protest. 'I don't think it was very wise to invite the Scotts with Y, Sophie,' he said. 'You know he likes to have people thoroughly vetted before he meets them.'

'Don't be so silly, Charles,' she told him. 'I've vetted them. Super people. In any case, Stephen's a well-known author, highly respectable. And keep your eyes on the road.'

Meanwhile Forbes and Leila – on two separate occasions, both times in Puerto Banús – had spotted Zakhr, the man whose thumbs Forbes had ripped out of their sockets. Once he was being driven in a maroon Opel Astra. The second time, his thumbs out of splints but heavily bandaged, he was playing backgammon at Da Paulo's, clumsy with the cup but managing to roll the dice.

So far, there were only two men on Forbes's

payroll in Marbella, Freddie Fraser and Luis Roldán, and they had had nothing to do. Freddie was in any case convalescing with his wounded arm, but even so he could be depended upon if needed.

'There's someone I'm going to need taken out,' Forbes told the cockney on the morning of his scheduled lunch with Sulman at the Sandhursts'. He was worried that, despite his beard, and his hair, which was a little longer than it had been and whose grey bits were tinted brown, Sulman's backgammon-playing heavy might recognize him. Or Leila, for that matter, even though she had gone blonde.

'Right out, guv'nor?' asked Freddie, stirring his coffee. They were sitting under a Martini parasol outside Bar Sport opposite the verdant central park on Marbella's main thoroughfare.

'He has to vanish from the scene. There mustn't be a body. If he's with someone else, he'll have to go too. If there's a car involved, I don't want it dumped anywhere. Sulman mustn't be alerted that there's anything up or he's going to dive for cover and never resurface.'

They both fell silent as a pretty girl walked by, her miniskirt flicking high up a bare, brown and shapely thigh with each step. It was amazing what a sexy piece of skirt could do to a conversation, even when the topic was murder.

'But he's gonna smell a rat in any case, ain't he?' asked Freddie, his eyes still on the girl, who was waiting for the little green man on the traffic lights to tell her it was safe to cross the road to the park. 'Heavies going on the missing list?'

'Not as much as he would if their stiffs turn up. These guys aren't that bright. You know that, and Sulman knows it. They might have gone on a bender, duffed somebody up and landed in goal. Or maybe they've been poached. It won't alarm him unduly.'

Halfway across the road, the girl fell laughingly into the arms of a young man coming from the park. 'Lucky bleeder,' said Freddie. He looked at Forbes and took a sip of coffee. 'Vanishing act,' he said. 'We can garage the motor, if there is one, and lock the geezers up somewhere until the job's done.'

'They're not worth the trouble. Blow them away.'

Apart from the vintage Bentley, there were just three other cars on the Sandhursts' drive when Forbes and Leila arrived for lunch just after two: a white Mercedes 600, a white 280SL, and a different black-windowed Cadillac from the one which had dealt death to three of Forbes's men. Forbes supposed, correctly, that the usual cars were having their damage repaired. As he swung his legs out and straightened from his hired BMW 750i – the expense of which Mullah had reluctantly agreed to since it fitted his supposed status – he avoided any direct eye contact with the men who were hanging around the drive.

The Cadillac doors were open, and inside a card game was in progress. Three men were squatting on a lawn, chatting, and two more were leaning on the 600, smoking. One of those two had bandaged thumbs.

You're going to die, Thumby, thought Forbes, sensing Zakhr's eyes on the backs of Leila's black-skirted legs as he walked her up the flight of steps to the Sandhursts' front door. As he tugged the chain on the old ship's bell, the grim thought brought him a certain amount of satisfaction.

In the spacious, slightly tired drawing-room, Sheikh Sulman and Lord Sandhurst rose to greet them. In deference to the heat, the sheikh was wearing neither jacket nor tie, but he had on one of his habitual little round, flat silk hats, this one a pale-rose colour and studded with precious stones.

'A great pleasure, sheikh,' said Forbes, tingling with excitement, and thinking: and you're going to take a little trip to Kuwait very shortly, as he stared the man levelly in his dark, piercing eyes with their *café con leche* whites. Deliberately squeezing the skinny hand hard, he was surprised to find the pressure returned. He smiled his love-me-you-bastard smile and said: 'Lord and Lady Sandhurst have said wonderful things about you.'

'Lord and Lady Sandhurst are most special people,' replied Sulman.

Lady Sandhurst kept steering the conversation on to the topic she thought the sheikh most appreciated: money. While she was recounting one of her favourite anecdotes about how Paul Getty had once stuck her with a taxi fare because he never thought to carry cash with him, Forbes noticed that Sulman kept darting Leila furtive little glances which seemed to denote more than a little sexual interest. All right, buster, he thought.

'Tell me something, Sophronia,' said Sulman when her story was done, 'why would someone as rich as Paul Getty take a taxi? Why would he not go everywhere in a chauffeured car?' Most of the question was addressed to Leila, who gave him several encouraging little smiles. Play this up, Leila, she told herself. Play it up for all its worth. There's half a million quid at the end of it.

'I can answer that one,' said Sandhurst. 'Paul was the meanest little shit in trousers. Chauffeur? He even cleaned his own shoes!'

The sheikh's new female companion laughed along with the rest of them. But she had said very little because her knowledge of English was paltry. Her name was Yolanda, she was chubby and Spanish and seemed to have gypsy blood in her veins. Sulman liked her because she appeared to genuinely enjoy his deviant brand of lovemaking, not faking pleasure like so many of her predecessors. But as the meal progressed it seemed he liked Leila even more.

From Forbes's point of view, the lunch went exceedingly well. Being face to face with the man he was contracted to spirit away to Kuwait for interrogation and certain death, exchanging conversation with him and even a little banter – though the sheikh's sense of humour was strictly limited – brought to him the keenest excitement. Had the slightest opportunity presented itself he would have loved to have whipped Leila away somewhere for the quickest of quickies.

The perverse need – perverse, that is, from the angle of its arousal – subsided with the departure of Sulman, who, Forbes had noted, had never been addressed to his face as Y. Forbes and Leila stayed on for another drink.

'He's rather nice,' observed Leila, half meaning it.

'Oh ho,' chortled Sandhurst. He was well in his cups.

'You'd better watch it, Stephen,' Sophronia said gaily. 'Did you see the way he kept looking at her?'

'He should be so lucky.'

'And you shouldn't be so bloody cocksure of yourself,' grinned Leila. 'I might get to like the idea of having my own runabout jet.'

He laughed. Then he said to Lady Sandhurst, his timing, he thought, just about perfect: 'You don't suppose . . .?' He shook his head. 'No.'

'Suppose what, dear?'

'Oh, I was just wondering if you could wangle us an invitation to his house with you. His character interests me far more now we've met.' He smiled crookedly at Leila. 'He's given me a sort of an idea.' Looking frankly at Sophronia, he added: 'I suppose it's a little too much to ask?'

She put her hand on his knee, her latest closest friend. 'Don't be so silly, Stephen. Of course it isn't too much to ask. I'll see about it tomorrow.'

He remembered the broken-thumbed heavy. 'That would be just great. But there's no hurry. We're busy until the beginning of next week.'

'Better watch the little lady with him, old feller,' blustered Sandhurst. 'Got a bad case of the hots for her, if you ask me.'

Which is one very good reason for him having us over, old feller, thought Forbes with some satisfaction.

22

They were digging a hole. Freddie Fraser and Luis Roldán had hired a big, yellow mechanical digger, and dressed in overalls, they were making a bloody great hole with it.

As the crow flies, it was not far from Chez Sandhurst, this hole. It was by the side of the dead-end road to the mountain village of Istán, a couple of kilometres up it before it began to snake past the reservoir which fed that part of the coast – and all the golf courses – with water.

To anyone who might have been remotely interested, the digging appeared to be an official something or other. They had marked out an area the size of the double-decker bus laid on its side, with iron poles and red-and-white-striped plastic tape, leaving one end open, and they were excavating within it. They had chosen the side of the road rather than somewhere more hidden away because people tended to take less notice of something going on under their noses than they would a similar activity stumbled upon in an unlikely area; and they had selected this particular winding road because of its bends, because there was little traffic on it and because it was close to the coast.

Nevertheless, caution prevailed. You could hear a car coming around the hidden bends from a long way off, and whenever one approached the two men would sit down with their backs propped against the machine, on its side furthest from the road; people took even less notice of a parked mechanical digger than a working one.

They were a fine team these two, and they liked and admired one another. Freddie remembered most clearly the incredible sight of the hilt of a throwing knife seeming suddenly to sprout from the eye of the Arab in the boot of the Cadillac who had shredded his arm. Roldán recalled the stoical attitude of Freddie as, spouting arterial blood, the man had carried on uncomplaining with the job in hand until they were clear of the mini-massacre.

As the afternoon sun burned down on them, making Freddie sweat like a pig and turning his face blotchy red but apparently having no effect on the Colombian, their hole grew deeper and deeper and the pile of stony mountain soil by its side grew higher and higher.

The same team working on the hole had already identified the man with the bandaged thumbs. He was a backgammon freak, and played almost every day at Da Paulo's during his free hours. He would arrive at about four in the afternoon, driven by his pal in the Opel, pick a game – there were usually two or three going on – and join in. The pal did not play, but he appeared most content to just sit, sip Coca-Cola and watch.

Noticing this, Freddie and Roldán had no idea that Zakhr – who, being an Arab and backgammon being a game of Arabic origins, thought he was a master player – was being taken on a long, slow ride to the cleaners by the affable professional players who preyed on such as he. His biggest weakness was that modern-day American invention, the cube with which the stakes could be doubled and redoubled and which he understood poorly. This device was costing him dearly – but at least he continued to breathe.

It was Friday evening. The heavy had dropped a bundle and was in a foul mood. He had been having such a shit-awful run lately, the bloody dice were always against him, his opponents, the whoresons, all rolled better than him, and so on. Thus had his pal to suffer as he drove them towards the eastern exit gate of the port.

There was a little red sentry-box affair at the

exit, occasionally but not that often manned by an official who might have a perfunctory look in the boot of a car. It had, in fact, been manned today but the hapless inspector of customs, at the moment when the Opel reached it, was bound hand and foot and gagged behind its closed door.

Roldán, in a smart peaked cap and an open-necked, clean white shirt with the word 'Aduana', 'Customs', stitched on the pocket in blue – Leila was a very neat sewer – stepped smartly forward from the box, holding up his hand for the Opel to stop as Freddie, similarly attired, moved in on the other side of the car.

The driver opened his door and stuck a foot out. With a shake of his finger Roldán indicated that he should stay inside. Opening the rear doors of the car, Forbes's men peered inside in the time-honoured procedure of customs officials – with one major difference: those gentlemen are not in the habit of slipping on to your back seat and sticking guns into your neck.

'Drive,' said Freddie, to a man suddenly gone cold with fear.

Sheikh Sulman's heavies were obliged to travel in the Opel Astra along the N340 to the turn-off for Istán, past the Sandhursts' villa and all the way up the winding mountain road until they arrived at Freddie and Roldán's big hole. The digger was sitting next to it, its business end with its teethed scoop hanging in the air on a crooked arm making it look like some yellow prehistoric beast.

It was still daylight – it did not start getting dark at that time of the year until almost ten. Because they had calculated it was going to be light, Forbes's men had earlier rigged a canvas on the road side of the hole, a metre and a half high so that no passing motorist could see into it. Everything was as they had left it.

Freddie made the driver park sideways on to the road with the car's nose facing the hole. The pit was a metre and a half deep – just enough – and there was a steep ramp down into it.

The heavies sat very still, silently staring into the hole in growing, dreadful comprehension.

As Freddie and Roldán waited for a car to pass and then listened to make sure that there would not be another for a minute or two, Zakhr decided on action. He lurched back across the seat, trying to grab for Freddie's silenced pistol.

The cockney put a hole all the way through his head. The bullet shattered the windscreen as Roldán killed the driver, who was starting to scream. The two scrambled from the car.

Opening the front door in a hurry because there was the noise of a motor cycle roaring down the hill, Roldán reached between the bodies and let off the handbrake. Freddie pushed the Opel into the hole. It rolled down, smashed into the far earth wall, bounced on its springs and settled down. Seconds later, the biker screamed by without even turning his head.

Speedily, the two men changed into the over-alls they had left with the Vespa dropped off at the hole earlier in a van. Then, resting each time a vehicle passed by, they set to work filling in the king-sized grave.

By the time the sun began to sink behind the mountains, the Opel and its grisly contents were buried, the ground was smoothed over and the surplus earth was spread over a wide area. Roldán took down the screen, untied the plastic tapes and uprooted the iron spikes, leaving all the items on the seat of the digger which he would return as agreed to the plant-hire company in the morning.

The late evening shadows were stretching long, as the assassins, legally attired in crash helmets, Roldán driving the Vespa, cruised leis-urely back down the mountain road, enjoying the fresh smell of the air.

23

Sitting in the back of the Bentley as he and Leila and the Sandhursts approached Casa al-Riyadh, Forbes suddenly found himself feeling just a little unreal. It was as if he were watching himself in a movie; there was the gorse bush behind which he had hidden to shoot out a security camera and from where he had seen the unfortunate drunk get gunned down; on the far side of the wood was the pine tree where he and three now dead men had listened in to Sulman's telephone; and now they were passing the corner of the cypress hedge where he and Leila had been playing tourist when his film had been destroyed by the man with the dislocated thumbs so recently destroyed himself.

The sense of unreality intensified when Lord Sandhurst drew the car's noble nose up to the gates, tooting his horn unnecessarily as the elephants began to swing apart.

'Bet you've never seen a pair of gates like that

before, what, old boy?' Sandhurst said over his shoulder.

The irony was so intense that Forbes wanted to laugh aloud. Leila, repeating her remark on first seeing the gates, said: 'They're African elephants, not Indian.'

'I know,' said Sophronia. 'You can tell by the ears.'

The elephants closed behind them and a second set of gates which Forbes had barely glimpsed before began to open. No design on them, heavy, painted green, they were just as massive and strong as the front ones.

'Tiresome bloody business,' grumbled Sandhurst. 'Like getting into Fort Knox.'

And there it was, sprawling before them, the house which Forbes knew every inch of from the air but had until this moment seen very little of from the ground. It was in a sort of hacienda style, but somehow it did not appear quite right; various sections seemed to sit uncomfortably in the wrong places, as if the original building had been torn apart by some monster of a child and put back all wrong.

The giant swimming pool lay quiet and still, reflecting the deep-blue sky of the dying day. Over to the left on its pad sat the Chinook which Sulman used to ferry guests to and from the airport. There were very few cars on the drive, which puzzled Forbes; he was not to know that there was a garage beneath the house crammed with them.

'Christ,' he muttered as Sandhurst parked the Bentley near the beaten-copper front doors.

Sophronia's eyes followed his astonished gaze to the out-of-place chandelier turning very slowly on its chain, speckling the doors and the entrance patio with tiny, moving lights. 'Quite,' she said.

'What is it, a *palais de danse*?'

'*Danse macabre*, Stephen. *Danse macabre*.' She was joking, but Lady Sandhurst's remark was very close to the truth.

Forbes's sense of unreality lingered on. As the little party neared the doors they opened with no visible assistance. 'There'll be the usual reception committee,' stage-whispered Sandhurst. 'You'd think we were armed and dangerous.'

With his hands tucked in his jacket pockets, succeeding in presenting a thoroughly relaxed appearance, and wearing the identical banker's outfit he had last put on to pick up his unforthcoming fee for abducting the man with whom he was about to dine, Forbes was nevertheless taking in every detail of his surroundings. He noticed the security cameras on the walls of the house, two over the doors, and, behind the fish-pond in the semicircular entrance hall, the six large, unwelcoming men with bulging shirts.

High up, where the foyer wall joined the sort of corniced ceiling which belonged in a Victorian house rather than a mock hacienda, were more security cameras, smaller than those outside. In a passageway were yet more little cameras and two armed men.

Sheikh Sulman had on a candy-striped shirt, trousers the shade of green preferred by Irish football supporters, gold slippers, and this time his silk hat was cream. As Sulman shook Forbes's hand in his hideous drawing-room, not appearing over-pleased to receive him, Leila's impression of the two of them together was that the sheikh looked like a small-time Pakistani shopkeeper seeking a loan from his bank manager.

But Sulman's attitude as he greeted Leila underwent a dramatic metamorphosis; his face broke into a delighted smile, and he clasped both her hands in his and kissed her smackingly on both cheeks. Slightly repelled by his garlicky breath, she did not let it show. Producing her prettiest smile, as the hand-clasping went on for longer than protocol called for, she gave the sheikh's fingers what could only have been interpreted as a sexually encouraging squeeze and fluttered her eyelids at him. Forbes had that afternoon been lewd in his instructions to her in this respect; if the guy looks like he's getting a hard-on over you, he had told her, stroke it.

And that was exactly the way Sulman behaved. So, metaphorically, all through a dinner with enough sumptuous food on display to feed a multitude though the diners numbered only fifteen, Leila stroked.

The sheikh was at his customary position at the head of the table, with Leila seated on one side of him and Sophronia the other. Forbes, having intended to inflict his most lovable persona on his victim, found himself too far away from the man to do so. He was facing Lord Sandhurst, the two of them surrounded by unfathomable characters and obliged to make somewhat hesitant small talk. There were no other women present, not even the Spanish whore. Whoever these people, mostly eastern and one fat American, were, they weren't volunteering very much information about themselves.

But it seemed to matter not that Forbes was more or less out of contact with Sulman. Leila was making enough headway for two, chatting away nineteen to the dozen, and coming out with enough remarks laden with sexual innuendo to cause Sophronia to begin to have serious doubts about her intentions.

Good God, the gel's a little slut, after all, her ladyship was thinking as the meal drew to a close. She's leading Y on something rotten. This opinion she could be excused for holding, since Leila was doing exactly that; temporarily, the Forbes's half a million was in her crimson-nailed hands.

Leila was doing her job in admirable fashion. Unhappily, she was doing it just a little too well.

After dinner, the sheikh was in the habit of taking his guests from the dining-room either into his gaudy disco or to his mini-theatre to watch a movie. Not so this night. Paying constant close attention to Leila, he escorted her and Forbes and the Sandhursts on a tour of his premises. As they hovered around the french windows at the back of the house, with Lord Sandhurst sneaking a much-needed slug of Stolichnaya from his hip-flask, Sulman took Leila by the elbow.

'Why don't you show Stephen the garden, Sophronia?' he suggested. 'Meanwhile there's something I'd like Leila to see.'

Bet your life there is, thought Forbes, eyes watching them closely as Sulman took Leila back into the house. Forbes by now had a fairly clear idea of the interior of Casa al-Riyadh, and now he was obligingly going to be escorted over the gardens. So far he had counted twenty-three bodyguards. There were even more men, undoubtedly, but he could safely estimate the total strength at about thirty; formidable, but not an insurmountable challenge. However, if things continued along the same satisfactory route as they seemed to be following, it wouldn't matter a hoot about Sulman's army. Plan A would win the day.

'Here are the tennis courts,' Sophronia announced unnecessarily as she walked Forbes away from the house along a rose-lined footpath. They had left her husband behind. He had sunk into a recliner on the terrace and was swigging more of the booze prohibited in the house – bang under the eye of a security camera.

Forbes was not much interested in tennis courts. His gaze had fallen on a box-shaped brick construction. It was about the size of a ship's cargo container, there was a large ventilator grille in it and it was half covered with ivy. He managed to steer them close to it. There was no doubt: it was an emergency generator.

'Why are you walking around so bloody oddly?' Sophronia asked brusquely moments later as he tried to appear casual while pacing out the distance from the generator to the corner of a tennis court.

'Am I?' He grinned ingenuously. 'Sorry. It happens sometimes. My head starts working away on something in my book and off I go. Sorry.'

'Ah. The artist emerging.' She threw him a look which seemed to say: I'd like to have you stuffed and displayed in a glass case in my drawing-room.

Meanwhile, the sheikh had taken Leila upstairs and through a door padded with studded pale-cream leather into a most extraordinary room.

'I'm not sure that I . . .' she began as her eye fell on a huge, circular, black-silk-covered bed which dominated the middle of the room.

'That you what?' he asked, softly closing the door of the only room in the house except the toilets which was not covered by a video camera.

She forced a smile. 'Nothing, really. I was kind of wondering if you should leave the rest of your guests alone.' Shit, she was thinking, what am I worried about? You might be a man, sunshine, but I bet I could tie you in knots if I had to.

'They can take care of themselves for a while. I really wanted to show you my den. I thought it might amuse you.'

'Yes, well, very nice,' she said, glancing around. In fact it was in just as ghastly taste as everything else in the house. The walls seemed to be gold-leafed and were liberally spread with erotic prints. There were lots of big, pink-tinted mirrors and close to the bed there was a life-sized marble statue of a nude, muscular man and a petite, naked woman, performing the act of sixty-nine vertically; the woman's thighs were wrapped around the man's neck. On the black ceiling, above the bed and exactly the same size as it, was a gilt-framed mirror.

Leila did not know in which direction to look. She was hardly the prude, she immensely enjoyed things erotic, but she was feeling distinctly awkward alone with Sheikh Sulman in his gruesome bedroom.

'How do you like my sculpture?' he asked her, sexual embers glowing deep in the black of his eyes. 'I specially commissioned the artist to produce it for me.' He ran a caressing hand over the cold, smooth, female buttocks. 'Beautiful, is it not?'

It was. Vulgarly beautiful. 'Very,' she managed. She wandered to a window. Below her, in the gardens, Forbes had his arm linked through Lady Sandhurst's and they were strolling down towards the sea. Far off, the fish-attracting paraffin lamps of a small line of boats threw fractured pools of light into the Mediterranean as their engines chugged softly.

Sulman watched Leila intently as a knot of excitement grew in the pit of his belly. While not really plump enough for his taste, she oozed sexuality. The silver-sequinned evening dress she was wearing fitted her as tightly as the scales of a sensuous fish, clinging to every line of her body, outlining the curve of her buttocks as if she were naked. The little bitch, husband or no husband, had been asking for it all evening. His loins clenched as his eyes appraised her tight little behind. He wanted her badly. And he most especially wanted that delicious part of her anatomy. He moved in.

'Stephen and Sophronia won't be back for quite a while yet,' he said softly, putting his hands on her shoulders.

She went very tense, but she let the hands stay. 'Just what do you mean by that?'

He turned her around to face him. 'There seems to have been something between us tonight.'

Yeah, she thought, your rotten breath. More garlicky than before dinner, it washed over her face. 'I hadn't noticed,' she said. But she forced a weak smile. Act, stupid cow, play it up, she thought, it's just for a little while. You can bear it.

'I can't believe that. I think you did.'

'But we hardly know each other,' she told him, feeling, as she spoke the banal words, like an actress in a bad movie.

'It doesn't matter. I want you.' His eyes bored into hers. 'You want me.'

'Now, just a minute.'

She tried to wriggle away from him, but his

talon-like fingers had tightened on her shoulders. Christ, he was going to kiss her. Shit! Cool it, kid, let him. It's just a mouth. Lead him on to the point where he knows you're game for the sack, then contrive your way out of here on a promise before it goes too far. You're the bait, remember. He's the killer whale.

It was awful beyond belief, those thin, spittly lips on hers, the lousy smell of his breath, his trying to force his tongue through her firmly closed lips, his lumpy crotch squirming against hers. She managed to break away, gasping: 'It's too soon. Too soon.'

'Nonsense.'

He pulled her into him again, a hand groping her breast, another crawling to her buttocks, plundering, misinterpreting her wriggles as passion.

Stay with it, she shouted to herself. Stay with it just a little more, Leila, just a little more, then run. Play the guilt-ridden little lady, blubbering a bit, filling his ears with the promise of the ultimate prize; but not here, Mr Sheikh, sir. Not tonight with loving hubby strolling in your garden. Another day. When we've got to know each other better.

Sulman's hands and mouth gluttonously invading her, Leila froze. A couple of seconds more, that's all. Bear it for a few seconds more. Kiss him back. Respond. Then skedaddle.

But somehow, without her even realizing it until the sequinned dress had opened on her like a pea-pod, he had slid its hidden zipper down from armpit to mid-thigh and his predatory fingers were right there, hooking between her thighs, grabbing her crotch, fingertips probing her fine silk Dior knickers.

Christ, no!

She backhanded him. Little Leila lost her cool and swiped his leering face hard with her knuckles, her emerald ring cutting the corner of her lip.

The look he flung at her was a mixture of shocked disbelief and hatred. A woman – a fucking inferior shit of a *woman* – had dared to strike *him*! His hands curled into trembling fists, the lust in his eyes changed to fury.

As Leila clumsily zipped herself up, she thought he was going to hit her. But no: he simply stood there, pent-up rage surging through him, shaking from head to toe.

'I . . . I'm sorry. I'm sorry,' she stuttered. 'I didn't mean to, you shouldn't have . . . Oh, shit!' She'd blown it. She'd blown it to hell and back and there was nothing more to be said or done.

'Get out of here,' he grated at her through

clenched teeth. 'Get out of here, *puta*.' He used the Spanish word for whore. 'Collect your scribbling apology for a husband and leave before I change my mind and have you both exterminated.' He licked blood from the corner of his mouth as she backed towards the bedroom door.

He followed her, pushing past her, yanking the door open, grabbing her by the shoulder and sending her reeling through it.

Lurking at the end of the corridor was the inevitable heavy. Sulman blurted something in Arabic at him and the man came to threatening life. Moments later Leila found herself being hustled down the stairs as the bodyguard barked urgently at two other men, who hurried on ahead of them.

'Here,' said the heavy as they reached the goldfish pond. He poked her shoulder with a thick, menacing finger. 'You wait here.'

A few minutes later, a flustered-looking Lord and Lady Sandhurst and a puzzled Forbes, escorted by three none-too-friendly heavies, one of them with a hand on Sandhurst's upper arm, joined Leila in the hall.

Another man was hurrying down the stairs. 'Lord Sandhurst, Lady Sandhurst,' he said, poker-faced, 'Sheikh Sulman he ask me say you goodbye.'

The front doors were opened and they found themselves hustled out to the Bentley.

'What *have* you done, Leila?' asked Sophronia, in mild shock as she clambered into the car. 'What on earth have you done?'

24

Nobody could coax a word out of her on the
way back to the Sandhursts'. Leila sat in the
rear of the Bentley, her mind curled up in a
foetal ball, and said absolutely nothing. She was
feeling dreadfully soiled. She told herself over
and over again: it was only a touch, for Christ's
sake. She was a big girl – what difference was a
bloody *touch*? But it was not helping. She had
never felt so dirty in her life.

'Whatever it was, the damned girl seems to
have effectively wrecked our relationship with
Y,' observed Sophronia crossly as the Forbese's
BMW disappeared from their driveway.

'Done us a bit of a favour, then, what?' said
Sandhurst.

Leila refused to talk until they were back at
Ramptona.

'You really have to tell me, you know,' said
Forbes, following her to the bar.

Of course she did, but she hated the idea.
She did not even want to remember what had

happened. 'Fix me a drink, then,' she said, her first words since leaving Casa al-Riyadh. 'A stiff one.'

When she was done, Forbes found himself consumed with such a rage that this time *he* could hardly speak. Taking her in his arms, he held her very tight to him, so tight he could feel her heart racing. He caressed her hair, and muttered unintelligible little words about what he would do to Sheikh Sulman right that minute if he could get his hands on him.

'Fuck!' he said with finality.

She tilted her face up to his; he was wearing a confused, worried expression. 'Yes,' she said. No admonition for his language this time. There was no word in the English language more appropriate.

'I blew it,' she said miserably. 'Are you very mad at me?'

He looked at her in amazement. It was astonishing. You could know a woman as well as he knew her, she could know you, and yet she could still totally misunderstand you.

'At *you*?' he said. 'Of course I'm not mad at you, idiot.'

Hurriedly, he analysed his feelings. He detested the fact that the sheikh had had his hands where he did, but it was hardly the man's fault – Leila had flung herself at him. No, it was nobody's fault but his own, and he loathed himself for it.

'But I threw away half a million quid,' she was mumbling. 'I just threw it away.'

He rained kisses on her forehead, her cheeks, the freckle on her nose. 'I would not have had him put his oily Arab hand on your sweet little pussy even for a million quid,' he said. And he meant it. 'In any case, you hardly threw it away. All you did was to wreck Plan A.' He managed a weak grin. 'At what's going to be enormous cost to the government of Kuwait.'

Had the sheikh not responded quite so quickly, it would all have been almost laughingly simple. It would not even have mattered if the driveway of Ramptona had been overlooked by neighbours. All it would have taken was an invitation for dinner. Sulman would have come, if only because of the urge to press his randy attentions on Leila, whom he was convinced was more than willing for a roll in the hay with him. Just two other couples there: Freddie and Roldán with a pair of chicks hired from an escort service. No need even to contract any more mercenaries.

The sheikh arrives, let us suppose with the Spanish bit. Some of his men begin their habitual game of cards, while the others prepare themselves for their usual lengthy wait.

Hardly has Sulman arrived, his beady eye

lusting on Leila, when he is seized and shot full of sodium pentathol.

Sorry, ladies, we regret this very much, but here is an envelope for each of you containing more than adequate compensation for the inconvenience. The escort girls, the Spanish whore, the housemaid and her husband are tied up, sticky plaster is wrapped over their mouths, they are bundled away upstairs into a small bedroom and locked in.

The heavies are all out at the front of the house and on or around the driveway. Maybe one or two are near the pool but that makes no difference because Forbes has chosen a route to carry the unconscious sheikh down through the back patio and shrubs to a place previously opened up in the hedge diametrically opposite to and hidden from the pool area. There is a car waiting there. Freddie and Roldán heave Sulman on to the back seat, Leila and Forbes go in front, Leila driving. Sulman is spirited away to where the next stage in his transportation to Kuwait is prepared and waiting. Jackpot.

Much, much later, probably around midnight, by which time Sulman is airborne, one or other of the more intelligent of his heavies smells the proverbial rat; the house seems awfully quiet and the boss is overstaying his customary visiting time.

Investigation. But just a little too late.

Now this simple dream of a scheme was destroyed beyond repair — ironically enough because of Sulman's uncontrollable wave of lust.

Plan B it was, then.

25

It was no longer a question of reconnaissance. Forbes was not concerned where the man went nor when he went. He only cared that he would be at home in the early hours of the morning on the appropriate day, and all the information Forbes had gathered so far about the sheikh suggested that he was never out later than one.

Contingency or no, Plan B was a reality. It was an extremely complex, daring idea which Forbes's brain had been struggling to refine ever since his second agreement with the Kuwaiti ambassador. Having decided that a squad of twelve, not including himself or Leila – who was going to have a non-combative role – would be sufficient to pull off the snatch, he dispatched Freddie back to England to assemble a team of crack operators.

However, the weapons presented something of a problem. Forbes needed fire-power on the lines of that described to Awadi in London. Type 59 pistols were fine for a raid on a couple of cars but hopeless for this new plan. Since the Kuwaiti Embassy in Madrid, as expected, was unable to help, it was going to be up to Forbes himself, aided by Roldán.

Within a fortnight things were beginning to shape up. The ten new mercenaries hired to make up the squad were down on the coast and going through their specialized training for the assault. Each day they would meet on a deserted stretch of beach farther down the coast towards Gibraltar which had a house fronting it of similar size to Casa al-Riyadh. There, together with their boss, Freddie, Roldán and Leila, they would gather in swimwear late in the afternoons and go through their paces, their exercises appearing to be some strange and elaborate game.

The weapons arrived via a circuitous route. Forbes's initial call had been to a trusted contact in Libya, who had made contact with the supplier himself – a man who ran a car-rental firm in Cairo, Egypt. This man kept a stockpile of weapons on hand for the IRA, in a remote farmhouse near the peaceful and beautiful port of Bantry, in the Irish Republic.

Three days after the deal was sealed a private yacht from Bantry put into Estepona harbour, where it was summarily checked by customs police with a sniffer dog. Hashish or cocaine was their main concern, not guns, since this

stretch of the coast had more drugs pouring into it than perhaps any in the world.
The specially adapted yacht had been used
on several occasions. It had various brilliantly
contrived hiding-places which were unlikely to
be detected except in the case of a tip-off
and the resultant search, which invariably took
ships and vehicles apart bolt by bolt and then
even had the bolts checked to see if they were
hollow.

It was arranged that the yacht would remain in
port with the weapons untouched until the night
of the raid.

Forbes and Leila each adopted yet another
persona. They kept their first names, but he
became Steve Crispen, a producer of adverts
for television and she was Leila Halami, his
assistant director. They made contact in this new
role with a Marbella-based casting agent and
photographer, Marianne Nilsen, and employed
her to get together a large group of young-
ish teenagers. They visited Coin Film City, an
hour's drive into the hills from Estepona, where
they negotiated the services of a small film
unit.

Steve Crispen and the lovely Leila were going
to put together an ad for a popular soft drink,
Splitz. It was understood that the first night's
work was to be a test shoot.

Three weeks after the demise of its predecessor, Plan B had all its joints smoothly oiled and was ready to roll.

Forbes waited two more nights, for the moon to be at its slenderest.

26

The Rottweilers were going insane. Inside Casa al-Riyadh the two men in the security room were looking unhappy as they watched the screens covering the beach. Up in the tower a bodyguard was focusing the telescope on the sand at the bottom eastern corner of the gardens.

Three Range Rovers had parked behind the beach on the southernmost abandoned urbanization road. They had been packed with teenagers who were now streaming on to the sand, more than twenty of them. Two of the vehicles had windsurfing boards on their roofs which were being hauled down, while behind the third was a trailer with a small fishing boat on it. Inside the boat was a heap of yellow tarpaulin.

'What do you suppose this is?' asked the man on the telescope. He offered the eyepiece to his companion.

The Arab studied the scene. A young woman with wraparound sunglasses and punky strawberry hair streaked vivid green had begun to organize the teenagers into getting together a pile of driftwood. There were guitars and bongos and two hampers. Towels were spread out on the sand.

'Beach party,' decided the second man.

The Rolling Stones' 'Little Red Rooster' began to crackle into the viewing room through a microphone attached to one of the security cameras, competing with the howling of the dogs. One of the kids had gone right up to the wire and was trying to make friends with the Rottweilers, further enraging them.

'Go on, why don't you stick your finger through?' growled the watching heavy. 'Little sod.'

It was nine-thirty. The sun, a huge ball of orange, was beginning to slip behind the distant mountains. The Rock of Gibraltar, dominating the seascape, was turning magenta beneath the darkening sky, and the far-off coastline of Morocco – with its Spanish enclave of Ceuta a mountainous hump – was etched blackly on the skyline.

It was a superb night for a party.

Leila, while succeeding in hiding the fact under a mask of jolly efficiency, was stretched from the top of her punky head to the soles of her feet with bowstring tension. She was dressed in thin, olive-green leather jeans and a matching skimpy waistcoat over a white T-shirt. As she supervised the manoeuvring of the fishing boat on its trailer down to the back of the beach her toes were curling inside her trainers.

'Something stinks,' said one of the men in the monitoring room, as the pile of driftwood grew bigger. 'There's no wind tonight, so why the windsurfers?'

'Maybe they're hoping for some.'

'Oh yeah? But why go to the effort of getting the boards down from the cars? And what the hell's that fishing boat for?' The boat had been brought to rest a short way along the fence and the dogs were concentrating all their fury on it.

'Maybe we should check it out.'

As the man got to his feet there was fresh activity on the screens. Two large, white vans, led by a black-and-white Range Rover, were lumbering along the rutted old roads down towards the beach. Apart from the driver's cabs, they had no windows. The words 'COIN FILM CITY' were printed in big letters on their sides.

Everybody on surveillance duty in the house of Sheikh Yasser Sulman watched in puzzled fascination.

As night began to rapidly close in, the beach got busier. Technicians unloaded cameras, lights and reflective screens from one of the vans, cables were unrolled on to the sand from the other. A broad-shouldered man in a black T-shirt who appeared to be in charge of all this activity – the driver of the Range Rover – was standing under a security camera and kept saying, his voice clear in the monitoring room, his accent Australian: 'Will someone shut those fucking dogs up?'

'They're making a movie,' offered the man on the telescope.

'We'd better let the boss know.'

The sheikh had the Baroness von Pantz and several other luminaries of the jet set for dinner. Although it was far off, the barking of the dogs intruded into the dining-room and it was beginning to annoy him. The news that there was a film unit at the bottom of his garden was received with irritation – and a certain amount of suspicion, since it was now night. Whatever it was these people were up to, why pick there, of all places?

'Call the police,' Sulman ordered. 'Have their credentials checked. Meanwhile, lock the dogs away.'

A summons from Sheikh Sulman meant instant action from the Estepona police department. Within ten minutes a squad car was on the scene, its siren blaring, its lights blazing.

Lights were blazing on the beach, too. The

generator van was in operation and two heavy-duty studio lamps were trained on the area of the as yet unlit pile of driftwood, while Leila, with the aid of Marianne Nilsen, was having the kids sit around with the guitars and drums and was handing out cans of Splitz.

A BMW rolled up and parked. Its driver stayed inside.

The boss of the film unit, James Todesco, in fact one of the owners of the studio but down there to show them the spot and hanging around out of interest, flashed an infectious smile at the inquisitive policemen. 'Sure we have a licence to shoot,' he told them in perfect Spanish. 'Hang on.'

He went and rummaged around in a small, untidy pile of papers on the front passenger seat of his car. As far as Todesco was concerned this was a genuine night-time test shoot of an ad for a soft drinks company, and the licence had been properly applied for and granted. He produced the document, with a brief verbal explanation, and pointed to some crates of Splitz as one of the kids lit the bonfire.

The officers left perfectly satisfied, radioing in that all was in order.

Had either one of those policemen happened to glance under the heap of tarpaulin in the fishing boat, his attitude would have changed

271

dramatically. Had Todesco taken a peep, he would have been presented with one of the biggest shocks of his event-filled life.

Forbes sat quietly behind the wheel of the BMW until the police car departed. Then, his beard and moustache thankfully shaved away, his thick hair dyed silvery white, wearing black jeans and a black shirt with a red silk scarf knotted around his neck, he joined Leila. The colourful boss of the advertising company was with his assistant director and they were the only two people on that busy beach who were aware what was really going on.

Filming began. An establishing shot. A close angle on the bonfire scene. Cut. Rearrange the cameras, rebuild the fire. Another angle. Shoot again. And again. A tiresome, time-consuming business. After a while it became uninteresting to the point of boredom for any outsider watching it – which Forbes was partially depending on. The operation had been checked out as genuine, so no one was going to survey them non-stop, and the heavies in the monitoring room were not going to sit with their noses glued to the screens all night. They would play cards, or tiddlywinks, or with themselves – whatever they usually did.

One o'clock. Shooting was in full swing. The kids were having fun, knocking back sangria, singing, playing guitars and bongos.

The mercenary dressed from head to foot in black and with blackened face, buried deep within the pine wood, reported to Forbes by walkie-talkie that the elephants had opened and the guests were leaving. When the last car had disappeared down the N340 he moved stealthily off to his second post, where a hole had been dug uncovering the main electricity cable to the house. He lay flat on his belly in the long grass beside it, patiently waiting.

One-thirty. Sheikh Sulman was watching television on a home-movie-sized screen in the special viewing room with Carmencita, his Spanish whore. As he toyed with her breasts he was beginning to lust for her fat backside but was first waiting for a scheduled item dealing with Iraq and one of his most important clients, Saddam Hussein, on CNN World News.

An old, thirty-five-foot, wooden fishing boat, especially hired at a price its owner couldn't believe he was being paid, moved out of Estepona harbour. There were eleven foreigners aboard, no crew, just the owner at the helm. It headed east towards Marbella, staying one hundred and fifty metres from the beach.

One forty-five. Todesco had long since drifted off. The film crew were beginning to wonder when Steve and Leila were going to call a halt to what was only, after all, a test shoot. His eyes on the approaching lights of the fishing boat, his stomach a hard, tight knot, Steve ordered them to do another take, with the lighting changed. This time the shadows should be up-beach, the lights set up in the soft sand six metres from the gently lapping waves, pointing towards the fence.

One fifty-five.

The news item over, with a hand greedily clutching Carmencita's buttocks, Sheikh Sulman urged the girl before him up the stairs to his hideous bedroom as the fishing boat chugged its lazy way past the bottom of his garden.

On board the boat, its owner, having brought it at a slight angle closer to the beach, about a hundred metres off shore, watched in amusement as his bunch of lunatic foreigner passengers in their black-rubber scuba suits one by one pulled on diving masks with breathing tubes and slid down into the Mediterranean on the far side of the boat. It was a surprise visit to the party on the beach, Roldán had said, a birthday surprise. And the fisherman believed it − especially now that he saw there *was* a party on the beach. These foreigners were utterly crazy.

Leila entered the generator van with a plug, its black lead attached and trailing out into the night, in her hand as the eleven mercenaries swam strongly beneath the sea, only their breathing tubes breaking the surface of the water, towards the beach.

'Hook this up for me, will you?' she asked.

The technician frowned at the unfamiliar plug. 'What is it?'

She jumped on him. She did not mean to, but she was as nervous as a kitten. 'Do me a favour? Just plug it in?' she barked.

He did so with a dissatisfied grunt. Leila followed the lead back to where it disappeared within the furled sail of a windsurfer standing close to Sulman's fence. Propping her back to the fence, she carefully eased the essential piece of heavy equipment from its hiding-place within the sail. She watched Forbes, waiting for the moment which she knew to be very close.

One by one, on their bellies, the mercenaries crawled from the sea. They would be invisible to anyone still alert on guard duty within Casa al-Riyadh since they were buried in darkness behind the blazing studio lamps.

The kids were singing, the cameras rolling. Except for Forbes, no one noticed the men as, black shadows within black shadows, they pulled on passive night-vision goggles.

Forbes himself put on a pair of the PNGs.

He spoke calmly into his walkie-talkie. 'Do it.'

The man by the hole on the other side of the wood sat up and swung himself over it. Taking a firm grip of the rubber-insulated handles of his heavy-steel bolt-cutters, he positioned the razor-sharp blades on either side of the thick cable below him, tensed the muscles of his powerful arms and sliced through it.

The house and garden, and the fence, were plunged into darkness.

There would be approximately seventeen seconds before the emergency generator took over. As the teenagers, the camera crew and Marianne Nilsen looked on in shocked amazement, the mercenaries appeared apparently from nowhere and sprinted through the party and around the fire while Leila, using a thermic lance, cut a jagged hole about a metre across in the first wire fence. With the bright studio lights to guide her, she clambered through it and sprinted across the dog run to the second fence.

Forbes and nine of his men took Heckler & Koch G3 7.62mm assault rifles and a white phosphorus smoke grenade each from under the tarpaulin in the fishing boat. The remaining two stuffed Uzi 9mm machine-pistols into their belts and between them lifted a cumbersome M72 anti-armour rocket-launcher and three 60mm rockets from the boat.

In his bedroom, Sulman was crouched naked behind Carmencita who was nude from the waist down. They had been on their knees on his Persian carpet, Carmencita bent over the huge, round bed, the sheikh applying Johnson's Baby Oil to a part of the whore's anatomy it had never been intended for, when the lights went out. The occurrence did not bother him too much. Power cuts were an occasional nuisance in that part of the world and there were no untoward night noises to alarm him. In the dark, he continued undeterred.

There was no alert within the house. The bodyguards waited for the emergency power to be activated, unaware that a team of tough, determined men with Forbes leading them, ducking low and formidably armed, had rushed up the steep slope of the lower lawn and were hurrying through the garden towards the house, their world through their PNGs a dull, but clearly visible, green.

Leila was starting the engine of the BMW as the emergency generator kicked into action and the sirens, set off by the holes in the fences, shrieked, in turn arousing the dogs. The lights went on, and the powerful emergency arc lamps were activated by the same system which set off the sirens.

The night-duty heavies grabbed for their guns, while the sleeping majority woke up and fumbled for theirs.

The two men with the launcher planted it in the lawn, carefully aimed it, and sent a 60mm rocket with perfect accuracy at the emergency generator. There was a mighty explosion, a great ball of flame and the lights went out again. The charging men let fly their smoke grenades. These exploded with brilliant flashes and the garden just below the house, and the patio, were filled with dense white smoke. The men tore through it.

The sheikh had reached that stage of rampant lust where almost nothing could divert him from his purpose. Almost nothing. Fear of death was one of the somethings. The noise surrounding his house was incredible. Filled with terror, he broke off from his sodomy.

The shooting had begun. The bodyguards and their Smith & Wesson 459s and Walther PPK semi-automatic handguns were no match for Heckler & Koch assault rifles in the hands of highly trained soldiers of fortune. By the time Forbes and his men had stormed inside the house, every heavy who had been foolish enough to offer resistance was ripped to shreds and Forbes had lost only one man through a freakily lucky shot through the heart.

The mercenaries fanned out through the house, big torches hooked to their belts, searching for Sulman, who in a state of panic was struggling into his trousers.

It was Forbes who burst into the bedroom first, the nose of his assault rifle sweeping the room. Carmencita had barely had time to get off her knees. Sheikh Sulman, one hand on his half-mast trousers, was quaking in fear.

'Hi,' said Forbes brightly, with a wicked, triumphant grin. 'Remember me?'

The rest of the operation went as smoothly. They were obliged to blow away the gates with the rocket-launcher because the power cut had immobilized them, then Forbes's men dispersed into the Andalusian night and faded away, each following his own prearranged exit route. Forbes, Leila and Freddie took the drugged sheikh in the BMW to Ramptona.

Barely an hour later a red helicopter ambulance from Helicópteros Sanitarios landed on the drive. In a similar operation to the first one, but with the right man on the stretcher, Forbes and Sulman, bearing the same Kuwaiti passport as used before, were airlifted. This time the Kuwait Air Force plane was awaiting them at Seville airport, not Málaga.

Three hours after the raid, Sheikh Yasser Sulman was leaving Spanish airspace and heading for Kuwait.

Epilogue

This time, they got paid.

OTHER TITLES IN SERIES FROM 22 BOOKS

Available now at newsagents and booksellers or use the order form opposite

All at £4.99 net

22 Books offers an exciting list of titles in these series. All the books are available from:

Little, Brown and Company (UK) Limited,
PO Box 11,
Falmouth,
Cornwall TR10 9EN.

Alternatively you may fax your order to the above address. Fax number: 0326 376423.

Payments can be made by cheque or postal order (payable to Little, Brown and Company) or by credit card (Visa/Access). Do not send cash or currency. UK customers and BFPO please allow £1.00 for postage and packing for the first book, plus 50p for the second book, plus 30p for each additional book up to a maximum charge of £3.00 (seven books or more). Overseas customers, including customers in Ireland, please allow £2.00 for the first book, plus £1.00 for the second book, plus 50p for each additional book.

NAME (BLOCK LETTERS PLEASE) ....

....

ADDRESS ....

....

....

☐ I enclose my remittance for £_____

☐ I wish to pay by Access/Visa

Card number
☐☐☐☐☐ ☐☐☐☐☐ ☐☐☐☐☐ ☐☐☐☐☐

Card expiry date
☐☐ ☐☐